Storytime Connections

A Literacy Resource Guide

Produced by
KCET, Los Angeles

Published by
The International Reading Association,
Newark, Delaware

The International Reading Association, Inc., Newark, DE 19714

© 1997 by Community Television of Southern California

All rights reserved

Printed in the United States of America

01 00 99 98 97   5 4 3 2 1

Library of Congress Cataloging-in-Publication Data

Storytime Connections: A Literacy Resource Guide / KCET Los Angeles

p. cm.

1. Children--United States--Books and reading.

2. Storytime (Television program).

3. Children's literature--Bibliography.

I. KCET (Television station : Los Angeles, Calif.)

II. International Reading Association.

Z1037.A1S825 1996 97-577

028.5'34--dc21

ISBN 0-87207-178-2 (pbk.)

Storytime Connections has been developed to help you use the *Storytime* television series as a resource to supplement your everyday curriculum activities and especially your reading times. The guide contains background information about literacy as well as show summaries, book descriptions, and suggested follow-up activities. The guide contains the following sections:

SECTION A: Connecting to Literacy

This section includes background information about the television series, suggestions for using the series to encourage reading, an opportunity to reflect on childhood literacy experiences, and information about literacy and child development. Following these broader literacy-related topics, we have included specific suggestions for enhancing literacy every day in a child care and home environment, suggestions for involving families, criteria for book selection, and tips for reading aloud.

About *Storytime*	A-3
Media Literacy and *Storytime*	A-4
Ten Ways to Encourage Reading	A-5
Reflections on Literacy	A-6
Literacy and Child Development	A-7
Encouraging Literacy in a Child Care Environment	A-10
Everyday Fun with Literacy	A-14
Strategies for Involving Families	A-16
***Storytime*'s Guide to Choosing Good Children's Books**	A-18
Different Books for Different Ages	A-19
Tips for Reading Aloud	A-20

SECTION B: Connecting to Storytime Shows

This section contains a summary of each show, a description of each book read with the primary themes identified, and suggested follow-up activities. Activities have been broken into three types: a group activity or game, an arts and crafts activity, and an activity to do outside.

Program Descriptions and Activities	B-2
Episodes 101-140	B-2
Episodes 201-221	B-82
Episodes 301-310	B-124

SECTION C: Connecting to Resources

This section includes lists of all the books read on Storytime, organized in several different ways to help you easily access the information you need. Books are listed alphabetically and by theme. There is also a list of books that are especially recommended for younger children. (These books are also identified with two asterisks [**] throughout the guide.)

At the end of this section, you will also find a range of resources, a glossary, and a summary of research findings.

Annotated Alphabetical Booklist	C-3
Thematic Booklist	C-16
Social/Emotional Themes	C-16
Cognitive Themes	C-18
Cultural/Social Diversity Themes	C-19
Critical Thinking/Problem-Solving Themes	C-19
Types of Stories	C-20
Appropriate *Storytime* Books for 2- and 3-Year-Olds	C-20
Research Findings About Literacy	C-21
Glossary of Literacy Terms	C-23
Resources	C-25
Bibliography	C-27
Credits	C-27
***Storytime* Feedback Form**	C-28

iii

Letter from the Executive Producer

It is with great pleasure that I introduce our television series *Storytime* and this resource guide to you. *Storytime* has one important message for you: we hope that every day you will take time to read to children. Studies show that children who are read to come to school eager and ready to learn, with more self-confidence. As a child care provider, teacher, or parent, you can help children by simply reading one book a day together with them.

Storytime introduces viewers to a diverse group of books. You will see rhymes, interactive stories, realistic stories, nonfiction, fantasy, stories about animals, imaginary things, adventures, and fun. We expose viewers to a variety of writing and illustration styles, and we include books from many cultures. As the producer of *Storytime*, KCET Los Angeles is committed to bringing quality children's books to television and to supporting you in the important work you do every day with young children.

We hope you find the shows and this guide useful in your work, and we hope that you will share your feedback and reactions with us or your local public television station. And remember to keep a story in your heart.

Sincerely,

Pat Kunkel

Patricia Kunkel
Executive Producer

Storytime™

Section A
Connecting to Literacy

This section provides you with background information about the Storytime series and related literacy information. On the following pages you will find:

1

About *Storytime*
Background about the television series.

2

Media Literacy and *Storytime*
How a television show that models reading can encourage and support reading. Includes a parent handout on "Ten Ways to Encourage Reading."

3

Reflections on Literacy
An opportunity to think about your own experiences with literacy and how they affect the children with whom you work. Includes a "Literacy and Child Development" section that provides an overview of the stages that children go through in acquiring literacy skills.

4

Encouraging Literacy in a Child Care Environment
A visual approach with ideas and strategies to encourage literacy development. Includes the visual parent handout, "Everyday Fun with Literacy," which features suggestions for encouraging literacy development through everyday activities. Also includes "Strategies for Involving Families," which demonstrates ways to communicate with families and involve them in the child care environment.

5

***Storytime*'s Guide to Choosing Good Children's Books**
Some guidelines and criteria to help you select different types of books. Includes parent handouts on "Different Books for Different Ages" and "Tips for Reading Aloud."

Section A

Connecting to Literacy

Storytime is a television series, broadcast nationally on PBS stations. Check your local PBS station to find out the exact time and day of the broadcast in your area. There are seventy-one shows, each half an hour long. On each show, adults and young people, often celebrities, read quality children's books aloud to children. Overall, *Storytime* books reflect a diversity of styles, cultures, illustrations, themes, and categories.

> **The single most important activity for building the knowledge required for eventual success in reading is reading aloud to children.**
>
> U.S. Department of Education, *Strong Families, Strong Schools*, 1994

Storytime's primary goals are to encourage adults to read to children and to introduce children to stories. The series does this by showing a variety of adults, from television and movie stars to everyday people, reading a wide range of high-quality children's books to groups of children.

Other goals include:

- Exposing young children and their families to a diverse range of books and readers
- Conveying the joy and fun of reading aloud together
- Showing stories where social skills are learned, problems are solved effectively, expressive language is used, and many cultures are featured
- Demonstrating that television can be an effective tool for encouraging reading

Characters

KINO (performed by Mark Ritts) is a curious puppet who enjoys exploring the world around him and hearing stories. With the humor, mannerisms, and speech of a seven-year-old, Kino is self-assured and imaginative.

LUCY (Anne Betancourt) is Kino's friend. She is an artist whose creativity and imagination, along with her wealth of life experience and love of books and reading, spark Kino's interest.

MARA (Marabina Jaimes) is Kino's other adult friend who reads to him and his on-screen friends. Her knowledge of books captivates Kino, and their shared love of reading and stories makes them special friends.

A-3

Media Literacy and Storytime

Some people who love reading have criticized TV, and with good reason. Watching TV is easier than reading, especially for beginning readers, so when given a choice, some children will watch TV instead of choosing to read. We know that children who are heavy TV viewers tend to read less than moderate viewers because they use up their free time watching television rather than reading. When some children view a TV lineup filled with programs featuring the toys they play with, many stop using their own imaginations and just copy what they have seen the characters do on television.

Conversely, well-designed, age-appropriate TV can build imagination and encourage reading. In fact, when books are featured on TV, requests for them at libraries and bookstores rise dramatically. *Storytime* has been designed with the help of reading professionals to empower both children, and the adults who care for them, to experience the joys and adventures of books.

> Watching TV is easier than reading, especially for beginning readers. So, when given a choice, some children will watch TV instead of choosing to read.

 Storytime can help parents find books their children will like.

 Storytime models how to read aloud (and have fun doing it). The celebrity readers use different voices and lots of emotion. They invite listeners to react, and they stop to check for comprehension. This example is especially important for families who may not have real-life models for reading aloud. For them, the TV can be an important window on the world, and seeing their favorite stars reading can encourage them to think of reading as a "cool" activity. The variety of people featured on the program sends the message that all kinds of people (and even puppets!) read.

 Storytime's use of simple language and picture books can help those who are just learning English understand the story. The show can help adults who don't speak English introduce children to books that their English-speaking peers are reading.

 Storytime uses its cast to link real-life events to the featured story. This helps viewers see how reading relates to real life and how books can spark imagination.

 Storytime is a TV show that families can watch at home, and it can therefore facilitate a family literacy experience. Even adults who are not comfortable reading can curl up on a couch with a child to watch *Storytime*. By watching with children, adults send the message that reading is important. Grown-ups can extend the value of the program by doing some of the things listed on the next page. In addition to using the ideas yourself, we encourage you to share the page with the families you work with.

Ten Ways to Encourage Reading

You can use your television to get your child excited about reading. Here's how:

WATCH programs that feature books, like *Storytime*.

FOLLOW UP by reading aloud the books you have seen on *Storytime*.

EXPLAIN to the children that they can ask for (and get) the books they have seen on *Storytime* at the library. Help your children get library cards, and, with the librarian's help, show them how to find the books featured on *Storytime*.

CONNECT what you see on TV with real life by reading related books. For example, if you watch a baseball game on TV, have a baseball book ready for a bedtime story that night. If you need help finding a book on a particular topic, ask your librarian. You can also use Section Three at the end of this guide to locate books by theme.

HELP your child learn the difference between "beginning," "middle," and "end" by choosing events from a TV program you have watched and asking your child to tell you when in the story each event happened.

POINT OUT every time someone is reading on a television program. Remember that people don't just read books or newspapers. They also read street signs, storefronts, notes left on refrigerators, shopping lists, invitations, mail, scripts, computer screens, and more. Make a game of spotting people on TV who are reading and/or noticing all the things that need to be read.

ENCOURAGE children to make up their own stories by using the characters they see on TV. This not only helps children get ready to understand other literary concepts like setting and character development but also helps develop imagination. Figuring out what a person would do in a new situation develops a basic understanding of character.

LIMIT TV viewing time. Some children watch so much TV that they don't have any time left to read. Set aside some time each week as reading time (when the TV stays off).

CHOOSE TV programs designed for your child's age. Programs like *Storytime* choose their language carefully, not only so children can understand, but also to introduce new words at a pace appropriate for young learners. That kind of programming helps expand your child's vocabulary.

VIEW actively. Talking about what you see can help your child develop language and critical thinking skills. You can also use some of the same techniques you use when reading. If you watch from videotape, pause and ask children what will happen next. Or retell a program's story, but make up silly endings and let your child correct you.

Reflections on Literacy

Whether we are conscious of it or not, we convey messages to children all the time — messages about who we are, what we stand for and against, and how we feel about various issues, including literacy. Growing up, some of us received positive messages about literacy and the value of reading; some of us received neutral or, in some cases, even negative messages.

Because you are a role model at all times, letting children know what you think and feel about reading is important to keep in mind. You may find it helpful, too, to consider the following questions as you think about your own experiences with books and reading. Reflecting about your own experiences with reading can help you understand what messages you are sending to children and why. Conveying positive messages to children about books and reading can help them build positive attitudes about literacy.

AS A CHILD AT HOME

- Do you remember being read to as a child? What sounds, sights, smells, feelings do you remember from that experience? Who read to you? Was it always the same person?
- Did you see your parents or other family members reading? Did you read for pleasure as a child?
- How expressive was your family verbally? Who were the storytellers in your family? How did people react to their stories?
- What kinds of books were in your house when you were growing up?
- What other kinds of literacy activities took place in your home growing up? For example, did your family sing songs or play board or word games?
- What messages (stated or unstated) did you get about reading? How did those messages affect your attitude toward reading?

AS A CHILD AT SCHOOL

- What do you remember about learning to read?
- How easy or difficult was it for you to read?
- How did you feel about required reading for school?
- Were there any books that you liked to read?
- What kinds of books did you like to read? Why?

AS AN ADULT

- How do you feel about reading now?
- Do you still like the same kinds of books you liked as a child? Why or why not?
- Do you read for pleasure now?
- When do you read? Where?
- What messages about reading do you send to the children you care for?

Literacy and Child Development

> Provide all children with support, encouragement, experiences, and guidance so that they move through their literacy development in their own way and at their own pace.

Children learn to speak, read, and write in order to express themselves, communicate, gain control over their environment, and socialize. They learn by example and by their own attempts to express themselves in their everyday lives. Literacy develops as children move through a series of steps, sometimes simultaneously, each necessary for success.

Children begin by exploring books and seeing how print works. They then become aware of print in their environment. Children first read through memory and later are able to identify individual letters and words. As they discover the connection between letters and sounds, they begin to use this in their writing and decoding of print. They continue to build language skills and eventually, somewhere around the first grade, become more interested in and excited about the specifics of print and language.

Watching *Storytime* can help children with literacy development. It allows children who are visual learners to respond to the pictures and children who learn best by listening (auditory learners) to respond to the sounds and voices. Combining viewing with follow-up activities will allow those who learn best by engaging in hands-on experiences (kinesthetic learners) to learn in their own favored style.

Reading and writing skills can emerge at any age, but you can look for general markers. The stages outlined here are not necessarily tied to the ages listed, since all children are different and develop at different levels. Provide all children with support, encouragement, experiences, and guidance so that they move through their literacy development in their own way and at their own pace. Children need to feel that they are successful, whatever their achievements are.

Literacy and Child Development

STAGE 1

Pre-Kindergarten Children

- Explore books and "read" through memory.
- Benefit from listening to adults read aloud, tell stories, and model reading and writing.
- Develop emotional connections with books.
- Develop language skills through pretend play and fanciful and detailed storytelling.
- Use storytelling to help their understanding of narrative development. (Storytelling is a rich experience in dialects, accents, and cultural styles. Understanding and celebrating these styles increases motivation and honors the child's cultural background.)
- Understand that writing is symbolic. (This stage is similar to "babbling" in speech development. Children might scrawl a single mark on a dozen sheets of paper as their "signature.")

STAGE 2

Kindergarten Children

- Can pick up their favorite books and "read" the story from memory.
- Write stories and books relying heavily on detailed and elaborate drawings to convey meaning.
- Begin using print and start to decode print.
- May practice forming letters of their name.
- Have an increasing awareness of environmental print such as Exit signs and can recognize symbols like a stop sign.
- Start to write a string of capital letters and ask adults what it says (example: MPRMRHM).
- May turn the pages of books and tell the story from memory or use the pictures as cues. (They are not attuned to the print at this point. Their attention is focused on understanding the meaning of the story.)
- Pretend to take orders at a restaurant.

> Teaching a child to love reading is a process that can start long before he or she knows an "A" from a "Z."
>
> Arlene Eisenberg, Heidi E. Murkoff and Sandee E. Hathaway, *What to Expect The Toddler Years*, Workman, 1994

STAGE 3

First-Grade Children

- Write simple letters and notes.
- Represent a word by half of its consonant letters, usually the initial and final consonant. RKCRBKD translates into "Our car broke down."
- Are organizing concepts about print in their reading, less so in their writing.
- Understand that print has meaning.
- See directionality; know that print is read from left to right in English.
- Know that books have a beginning and an end.
- Have some recognition of punctuation, letter concepts such as the first letter of a word, single letters in words, and capital letters.
- Build on their understanding that letters represent sounds and now see that more than one or two sounds are recognizable.
- Begin to use vowel sounds in their writing.
- Can name the letters but are still working on forming rules for using them.
- Choose letters by their sounds. Invent their own spelling (example: GAGIN = dragon).
- Are increasingly influenced by environmental print in their spelling.
- Are easily understood when they speak.
- Practice speech in long, detailed storytelling.
- Still do not match the print on the page in their oral reading, although they are getting closer.
- Are learning letter names, can discriminate between letters and numbers, and are recognizing their own names and a few words.
- Become increasingly concerned with reading exactly what is on the page. (They are now in the transitional stage of spelling and are beginning to read. These young readers focus on decoding single words.)
- Overgeneralize the rules they are learning in both speech and writing, such as "eated" and "buyed." (As children progress toward the next stage, their writing contains an increasing number of correct or "book" spellings.)
- Express ideas in sentences at the end of this phase.
- Have pictures and words in their stories, and their sentences begin with a capital letter and end with a period. Some may even begin to use blends (pl, br, at) and vowels.
- Need to share their stories and receive responses.

A-9

Encouraging Literacy in a Child Care Environment

Music & Blocks

This area would include a variety of musical instruments and audiotapes of songs and stories from many cultures and musical styles. Children can sing or listen to songs, and words can be posted on an easel. Include alphabet blocks so that children can experiment with letters.

Art Area

Some children more readily express themselves through art. Art gives children a medium to learn different ways of communicating. Include a wide range of inexpensive supplies — pipe cleaners, Popsicle sticks, nontoxic paint, markers, glue, different colors and types of paper, egg crates, and other recyclable materials. Display pictures of different kinds of art, from realistic to expressionistic. Hang children's art, and encourage them to talk about their own work and the work of other artists.

> Art activities can help children to recognize shapes and to make meaning of symbols — both prerequisites for learning to read.
>
> Ellin Greene, *Books, Babies and Libraries*, 1991

You can help children become ready to read by creating a literacy-rich child care environment. This means providing children with a safe and comfortable place to examine and explore a variety of print materials, exposing them to words and language in many formats, such as labels, signs, posted schedules, bulletin boards, audio- and videotapes, and of course, many kinds of books.

Science Area

Label items and encourage children to practice their language skills by reading, speaking, and writing. Include science books and magazines in this area. You can include plants or a terrarium.

Circle Time

This large group space provides many literacy opportunities. Use the calendar, the job board, the daily schedule, and the bulletin board, which posts announcements, invitations, special activities, and events. Circle time also lets children practice their active listening as well as their speaking. They can share events in their lives, reactions to activities, give book reports, or tell stories. Of course, this is the time to read together as group.

Housekeeping

This center provides you with the opportunity to expose children to a variety of cultures and materials from different countries. Imaginative play provides children with a unique opportunity to experiment with language and conversation. As with other areas, labeling items is a good way to help children connect words to what they see. Include food tools, baking items, clothing, and house cleaning equipment.

Book Corner

This area gives children the tools of literacy — books, magazines, paper, and writing instruments. Encouraging children to write and to share their writing with others helps them communicate effectively and builds their literacy skills. Teach children to enjoy receiving and sending letters by having a mailbox for each child (and the teacher).

Games

Games help children see that learning is fun and understand that literacy is necessary to play some games. Expose them to different kinds of games, from board games to card games to simplified versions of Charades, which all provide children with fun and exciting ways to learn about communication. Supply games that can be played alone as well as with groups. Use the television where children can watch particular shows or videos that you have preselected for them to choose from. Encourage them to actively view by singing along, acting out favorite parts, or talking about what they saw.

Outside

Taking field trips or playing outside helps children learn about the world around them. Literacy skills can be enhanced by pointing out signs and symbols, learning the names of trees and flowers, identifying colors of outdoor objects or names of locations, etc. Outdoor activities help make classroom learning come alive.

Everyday Fun with Literacy

You can help your preschoolers become ready to read by encouraging them to see themselves as readers when they identify letters or words, draw and label pictures, or recognize symbols, like stop signs. Everyday, you have opportunities to help your child enjoy being a beginning reader. Here are some ideas.

At Home

- Watch *Storytime* together, and talk about it afterward.
- Put magnetic letters on your refrigerator for children to play with. You can also cut letters out and post them with tape on the refrigerator.
- Post invitations, announcements, and simple labels where children can see them.
- Make pictures of favorite foods and label them.
- Let your child see you use recipes. Point out words to them.
- At snack time, make words out of finger foods such as alphabet soup, or letters with finger foods such as cereal pieces.

In the Neighborhood

- Look for letters that children know on signs or license plates.
- "Read" street signs together.
- Notice and talk about billboards you see.

Visiting Family or Friends

- Before leaving, draw a map and mark your route.
- After the visit, have your child send a thank-you note or picture that he or she has drawn.

At the Grocery Store

- Create a shopping list with your child. Items can be written or drawn.
- Have children identify product names that they know.
- At the beginning of each aisle, pick a letter of the alphabet to look out for. Count the number of times you see it in an aisle.

> If you read a lot, you are saying to your child that reading is important and enjoyable to you. However, it is your reading aloud to your child that is vital to her future development.
>
> Theresa and Frank Caplan, *The Early Childhood Years*, Bantam Books, 1983

At the Park

- Draw letters in the dirt or sandbox.
- Collect leaves along the way. Then go to the library to find books so that you can identify them.
- On index cards or squares of paper, have your child draw pictures of all the people, animals, equipment or things you saw at the park. Write the corresponding word on another card. Turn the picture cards upside down. Play a memory game to see how many the child remembers by showing and saying a word and asking the child to find the matching picture.

At the Library

- Have the child spend time looking at books they have picked out.
- Participate in a library story hour and attend the library's other family-oriented events.
- Get a library card for your child and check out a variety of books.

At the Zoo

- Create a list with your child of the animals you think you will see. You could also cut animal pictures out of magazines or draw them on the list. Help the child cross names off the list as you see each animal at the zoo.
- Name each animal you see. See if your child can guess what letter the name begins with.
- Have the child draw a picture of a favorite animal. Hang it in a special place.

A-15

Strategies for Involving Families

To be most successful with the children in your care, you must work closely and in partnership with their families. Developing a working relationship with parents and guardians can be difficult because there is so little time available for you to interact with one another.

Often communication gets squeezed into stressful moments like during the pick-up and drop-off of children. This is not usually a good time to discuss issues or ideas at length. However, as the primary educator and a caregiver in the child's life, it is important that you and the children's families are in communication. Here are some ideas and tips to help you out.

Communication

1. Let parents know what you need and expect of them.

   - *Tell them the best times and ways to communicate with you.*
   - *Have set times they can reach you.*
   - *Leave a clipboard near your entrance so that families can leave you notes.*
   - *Hold periodic conferences with families to discuss the child's progress.*

2. Be clear and direct about the philosophical approach and values that you promote in your program. Families need to know what is being modeled and taught to their children. Stating this clearly in the beginning can help you avoid uncomfortable situations later.

3. Send home a journal or sheet that communicates the daily events and activities each day. This will help families feel that they are a part of the child's day and will provide them with a tool for discussing and reading about the child's day together.

4. Let all families know when you are having guests come to speak to the children in your care or to do activities with them. Children are not always able to communicate complete information and can leave their families feeling uncomfortable and misinformed about what has taken place in your environment.

5. When you share ideas — orally or in writing — do so in ways that will not be received as judgmental. You and the families you work with must be able to communicate in order to support the children's learning. Avoid using language such as "you should" or "you ought to."

Ideas for Home

1. Notify families when special events will occur, and give them suggestions for books, audio- or videotapes, or other activities that they can use to help prepare or follow up with their children.

2. Invite members of your children's immediate or extended family to come in as guest speakers. It is good for children to see and interact with different adults modeling the use of a variety of literacy skills and cultural backgrounds. Guests can share something about their heritage, lead the class in a favorite game, read a favorite story, or help to cook a special recipe.

3. Ask families to share recommendations of their favorite children's books, magazines, and music. You can share everyone's suggestions with all of the families. You can even ask families to help you set up a class lending library.

4. Let families know when you hear about community events that you think might be enjoyable and beneficial to your students. Ask them to do the same with you. This is a great way for all of you to learn about and gain experiences with a range of people from throughout your community.

5. Share the "Encouraging Literacy in a Child Care Environment" section in this guide with families, and suggest that many of the ideas and suggestions can be applicable for homes.

> If we could get our parents to read to their preschool children 15 minutes a day, we could revolutionize the schools.
>
> Dr. Ruth Love, Superintendent, Chicago Public Schools, 1981

Guide to Choosing Good Children's Books

How do you choose children's books? Do you pick books that you loved as a child? Books that have appealing illustrations? Stories about particular issues? Fantasies? Animal stories? With more than 5,000 new children's books published every year, the selection keeps growing. Here are some things to think about when choosing books:

- **Story:** Children's picture books can be realistic, profound, whimsical, silly, or even absurd. They can incorporate poetry, folklore, myths, and songs. Memorable children's books also offer a chance to reveal new or different worlds, celebrate different cultures, or make a meaningful statement about an important social issue. Above all, books should be entertaining and tell a good story.

- **Illustrations:** Just like the stories, the pictures in children's books can be realistic, simple, colorful, stark, or detailed. The more knowledgeable you become about children's books, the more you will be able to identify your personal tastes. Introduce children to a variety of illustration styles so that they can discover their preferences as well. For very young readers, try to choose books with only a few words on each page.

- **Language:** As a general rule, the story should be easy to follow and have words that the child will be able to understand or learn. Younger children particularly enjoy stories that use rhymes or repetitive language.

- **Format:** Children's books come in all shapes and sizes. Often young children love tiny books, books made of hard cardboard, or books with tabs to pull and flaps to flip. Provide a variety of formats. Books with small and/or very detailed pictures are best to present on a one-to-one basis, while large formats work well when reading to a group.

- **Categories:** There are many different types of children's books — realistic fiction, fantasies, animal stories, and nonfiction. Try to provide a balance in the types of books you select. Many children enjoy reading books about a favorite hobby or subject — dinosaurs, baseball, ballet, etc. Biographies are also good books to share, inspiring children and often providing an important sense of history.

- **Resources:** Ask the children's librarian at your public library for book suggestions. Get a library card in the child's name, and let him or her choose books to borrow. Look for story hours at libraries or for story corners in bookstores where children are encouraged to read and browse. You can also order books through mail-order catalogs especially designed for parents and teachers.

Many good books about children's books are available. We recommend *The Read Aloud Handbook* by Jim Trelease (Penguin, 1995, 4th edition), *For Reading Out Loud!* by Margaret Mary Kimmel and Elizabeth Segal (Dell, 1991) and *The Early Childhood Years: The 2- to 6-Year-Old*, by Theresa and Frank Caplan (Bantam Books, 1983).

Have fun! Reading books with children is one of life's most pleasurable activities. Whether it's a snuggly book shared before bedtime, a calming book just before rest time, or a funny story to giggle over together, story time can be a special time to enjoy with your child or children. You can share your favorite childhood books, open new worlds, discover imaginary characters together, and encourage young children to develop a love of stories and reading.

Different Books for Different Ages

Children's developmental levels and interests vary greatly. The following list of types of books and subject areas is intended only as a guide. You know your child(ren) best, so pick and choose accordingly.

Continue reading to your child after he or she begins to read. Choose books at a somewhat higher reading level than your child's. Try reading chapter books, reading one chapter each evening.

BIRTH–1 YEAR
- Lullabies and songs
- Clear, bright, simple picture books
- One or two pictures per page to make it easier for baby to focus
- Board or plastic books with easy-to-turn pages

1–2 YEARS
- Clapping rhymes and knee bounces
- Wordless and word-list books
- Simple good-night books
- Sturdy, feely, scented, and squeaky books

2–3 YEARS
- Stories that repeat catchy phrases
- Sturdy pop-up and pull-tag books
- Short stories with few words and many pictures
- Stories about everyday events
- ABC, counting, color, and shape books

3–5 YEARS
- Non-fiction: dinosaurs, trucks, farm animals
- Simple folk tales
- Longer stories and more detailed pictures
- Books chosen by the child that are of interest to him or her
- Stories that can be acted out

BEGINNING READER
- Short stories, with few words per page, and pictures that match text
- Books that interest the child
- Real-life stories, simple biographies
- Joke and riddle books
- Simple magazines

Adapted with permission from the author, Beth Bockser, Families For Literacy Coordinator, Project Second Chance, Contra Costa County Library.

A-19

READING ALOUD

Try to read the book ahead of time to familiarize yourself with the story, characters' names, etc.

Read slowly and clearly.

Use gestures to enliven the story.

Vary the volume of your voice, and use a unique speech style for each character.

Pick a book appropriate for the mood and temperament of the listeners.

Be aware of the children's attention span. Stop reading when they lose interest.

One-on-one Reading Tips

- You can read to a child anywhere. Create a comfortable and quiet space to sit in.
- Let the child sit on your lap or sit close to you, whichever feels most comfortable for the child.
- Encourage the child to interact with the book itself by pointing to pictures, identifying animals or characters, asking or responding to questions, predicting what will happen, and/or turning the pages.
- Try to maintain physical interaction with the child through eye contact, acting out parts of stories, or making sounds.
- Allow the child to choose his or her own books some of the time.

Group Reading Tips

- Gather children in a circle around you. Be sure that everyone can see you and the book.
- Try to have eye contact with every child at some point during the story.
- Choose books with pictures that can easily be seen at a distance.
- If children have comments or questions while you are reading, try to acknowledge them briefly without interrupting the story. In a positive and interested tone of voice, ask them to try to save their questions until the end. Remember to follow up on their questions.
- Enjoy yourself! Children will respond to your enthusiasm and excitement.

A Blueprint for Reading Fun

A comfortable, quiet environment

A variety of good books

Feelings of warmth, enjoyment, enthusiasm, and involvement

Storytime™

Section B
Connecting to Storytime Shows

This section includes information about the first seventy-one Storytime programs. Each show has its own page(s), including the following information:

1
Show Number
This is the number to use with your local PBS station or the show's producers if you are referring to this particular show. (Note that the numbers go from 101-140 for the first season's productions, 201-221 for the second season, and 301-310 for the third season.)

2
Summary of Show
This is a description of what happens on the show and who reads each book.

3
Guest Readers
A list of the celebrity or other guest readers.

4
Books Read
This includes a detailed description of the plot of each book, and following that, in parentheses, the major themes. Note that if you see the symbol **, it indicates that the book is appropriate for younger (two- to three-year-old) children.

5
Storypicks
These are the books that are recommended (but not read) on the show. The book title and author are listed.

6
Activities
For each show you can choose from three simple suggested activities: a game or group activity, an arts and crafts activity, and an activity to do outside. Note that many of the activities, especially the games, can be played with families.

Section B

Connecting to Storytime Shows

SHOW NUMBER 101

Summary

Kino is very impressed by Lucy's abstract painting, and she promises to teach him how to paint, too. Mara reads them a book about a naughty little dragon. Then John comes in to read a book about a little polar bear and another about a little girl whose neighbor seems strange and scary.

Guest Readers

John Goodman

📖 BOOKS READ

Anna and the Little Green Dragon by Klaus Baumgart: Anna is having her breakfast one morning when a little green dragon pops out of her cornflakes box. He makes a big mess out of all the food on the table and sprays cocoa in her face, and Anna gets blamed by her mother. Her mother doesn't believe it could really have been a dragon until a mother dragon appears at the door looking for her son. (theme: fantasy)

Little Polar Bear by Hans de Beer: While on his first hunting trip with his father, Lars the polar bear is set adrift to sea on a piece of ice. A storm carries him across the ocean to a warm beach where he meets Henry the hippo. Together they set out to explore this new world. Henry takes Lars to the mountain to ask Marcus the eagle how to get home. The eagle sends Lars to Samson the whale, who carries Lars on his back to his icy home where his father is waiting. (themes: animals, adventure)

Rose Meets Mr. Wintergarten by Bob Graham: When the Summers move in to their new house, they fill the yard with flowers. Next door, at Mr. Wintergarten's house, there is no sun and nothing is growing. Rose Summer has been warned to stay away from the scary Mr. Wintergarten, but when her ball flies over the fence into Mr. Wintergarten's yard, she brings cookies and flowers to ask for her ball back. He turns her away crankily but opens the curtains for the first time. He steps outside and kicks the ball back to Rose, sending his slipper with it. She throws it back, and from then on they are friends. (themes: friendship, feelings [fear])

📖 STORYPICKS

The Adventures of Isabel by Ogden Nash, pictures by James Marshall

Roses Sing on New Snow by Paul Yee, illustrated by Harvey Chan

ACTIVITIES

Game
Pair people up. Ask each person to pretend that an animal is on their back who will transport Lars to their partner in that animal's special way. For example, a horse will carry him on its back, a snake will slither on the ground. Afterward, in a large group, individuals can share what kind of animal they thought of.

Crafts
Have half of the group draw animals and cut them out. The other half will draw people. Pair up a child with an animal and a child with a person and have them act something out, exploring the many ways in which the animals and people can interact.

Outside
Cut the tops off empty milk cartons. Put two inches of soil in each carton and ask each person to put in some grass seeds. Keep them outside (weather permitting), and water them daily. Optional: The kids can decorate their cartons by coloring paper that is glued to the carton. Make this into a literacy activity by helping children label their containers with their names.

SHOW NUMBER 102

Summary

Guest Readers

Lucy

Amanda Plummer

Kino, Mara, and the group enter dancing in a line. Mr. G reads an alphabet book in rhyme, and Lucy points out that the illustrations are collages. Amanda, noticing that her hat is like a collage, reads a book about a hat. Leaving for an errand, she asks Lucy to read a book about a boy who wants a dog. Kino also wants a dog, but his mother doesn't want him to get one. After the story, Amanda returns with a surprise for Kino — a new dog. She ran into his mother, who said it was okay for Kino to have a dog.

BOOKS READ

Chicka Chicka Boom Boom by Bill Martin, Jr. and John Archambault, illustrated by Lois Ehlert: A colorful collage of letters climbs up to the top of the coconut tree in a singsong rhyme. Once they get to the top, the tree sags over, and they all fall down. One by one, they dust themselves off and pick themselves up. (themes: alphabet, sounds)

Chicken Sunday by Patricia Polacco: Natasha spends every Sunday with her neighbors, Stuart and Ninnie, and their grandma, Miss Eula. Each week they go to church, where Miss Eula sings, and they pass the hat store, where she admires a special hat in the window. The children decorate eggs, which the hat store owner lets them sell, allowing them to buy Miss Eula her special hat. (themes: family, caring/concern for others, differences, friendship, resourcefulness)

Any Kind of Dog by Lynn Reiser: Richard really wants a dog, any kind of dog, but his mother says a dog would be too much trouble. She gives him a series of other kinds of animals that look like dogs, but none of them are really dogs. Finally, she gives in and gives him a real dog. It is trouble, but Richard thinks it's worth it. (themes: responsibility, animals)

STORYPICKS

Pole Dog by Tres Seymour, pictures by David Soman

Eeny Meeny Miney Mole by Jane Yolen, illustrated by Kathryn Brown

ACTIVITIES

Game
Play a variation of hide and seek. Hide colored eggs (see below), and then let people work together to find them. The game ends when all of the eggs have been found.

Crafts
Work together on decorating eggs. Hollowed-out eggs can be painted using markers, regular paint, or paint dipped in a vinegar solution. Have the children think about different ways in which things can be used.

Outside
Assign each child a letter of the alphabet, which they may wear on their chests. These can also be written on oak tag paper or cardboard and hung around the child's waist or on their wrist with yarn. With large, clear letters, spell out words on a sign. The children will then form a line to spell each of the words displayed on the sign. Possible words include friendship, animals, song, and chicken.

Summary

Guest Readers

Tom Selleck

Kino is upset. His relatives are visiting, and they are taking over his life. He has to sleep on the floor, he is being covered with kisses, and he can't find his Dustdobbin book. Tom reads a book about relatives then finds the lost book and reads about the Dustdobbin. Afterward, he reminds Kino that his relatives love him even though he is having a grumpy day. Then Valerie reads her son a picture book about a mother's love.

BOOKS READ

The Relatives Came by Cynthia Rylant, illustrated by Stephen Gammell: It is summertime, and the relatives pack up their car in Virginia and come up for a visit. They are greeted with hugs and kisses. They stay for weeks, help fix things, plant things in the garden, and get into everything. Finally it is time to go home and dream of next summer. (themes: family, sharing)

Five Bad Boys, Billy Que and the Dustdobbin by Susan Patron, illustrated by Mike Shenon: Billy Que and the Dustdobbin under his bed both hate brooms, so they get along very well. Then, one day Billy steps on the Dustdobbin's toes while getting out of bed. The Dustdobbin is so mad he shrinks Billy down to his size. Then five bad boys happen to find the little Billy. They make him a cap with a strap, a cup, and a bench, and make shade for him to sit in. When he grows back to his old size, he continues to leave useful things for the Dustdobbin and is careful where he puts his feet when getting out of bed. (themes: fantasy, feelings [anger], size)

Mama, Do You Love Me? by Barbara M. Joosse, illustrated by Barbara Lavallee: An Eskimo girl asks her mother a series of questions about how much she loves her. (themes: family [mother], feelings [love])

STORYPICKS

Something for Nothing by Phoebe Gilman

The Wild Woods by Simon James

ACTIVITIES

Game
Play a variation of "Simon Says" where each person in turns gives directions to the others in the group based on something that happened in the books *Five Bad Boys, Billy Que and the Dustdobbin* or *The Relatives Came*. For example, they could say, "Act like brooms and sweep the floor," then "Freeze." Then: "Plant things in the garden," then they freeze, and so on.

Crafts
Have each child make a coupon to give to a parent or caregiver. The coupon should offer help with a household chore, a kiss or hug, or something that the child wants to give to a special family member.

Outside
Just like the relatives planted flowers, plant bulbs in the fall or seeds in the spring. Make this into a literacy activity by drawing pictures of the flowers that will bloom and pasting the pictures onto Popsicle sticks. Place the sticks in the ground on top of the planted bulbs.

SHOW NUMBER 104

Summary

Guest Readers

John Ritter

Kim Karnsrithong

Guest John Ritter and his son talk about how they read books at home. John reads a book about a town where everything is connected. He talks with the kids about the need for things to work together and reads another book, this one about a meticulous, hardworking little boy who is followed by an elephant. Kim comes in to read a book about a little boy who is very connected to his teddy bear.

BOOKS READ

The Old Ladies Who Liked Cats by Carol Greene, illustrated by Loretta Krupinski: In a town on an island, there live old ladies who like cats. They let the cats out every night. This works out nicely because the cats scare away the field mice and start a chain of events that is affected when the mayor trips on a cat and then banishes the cats from their nightly walks. When the sequence is broken, the town is threatened, but balance is restored when the cats are let back out. (themes: cooperation, nature, resourcefulness, sequence of events)

Alistair's Elephant by Marilyn Sadler, illustrated by Roger Bollen: Alistair is a very meticulous and tidy boy. He enjoys his homework and his chores and organizes his life very well. One day, he visits the zoo, and as he returns home discovers that an elephant has followed him home. He gradually learns to live with the elephant for the week until he can return him to the zoo the following Saturday. But on the way home from there, a giraffe follows him home... (themes: fantasy, problem-solving)

Ira Sleeps Over by Bernard Waber: Ira has been invited to sleep over at his friend Reggie's house for the first time. He is afraid that Reggie will think he is a baby if he brings his teddy bear, but he is afraid to sleep without it. Ira decides to go without his bear. Then, after an evening of fun, he learns that Reggie, too, has a teddy bear. After Ira runs back for his own bear, they can all fall asleep together. (themes: feelings [fear], friendship)

STORYPICKS

What's Under My Bed? by James Stevenson

The Great Kapok Tree: A Tale of the Amazon Rain Forest by Lynne Cherry

ACTIVITIES

Game
In small groups, play dominoes to see how important each piece is to the whole game.

Crafts
Have each child make a chain by tying together different colored pieces of yarn. Join these together and make a giant "necklace" or "belt." Show what happens if one of the children removes his or her chain.

Outside
On a walk or in a seated group, ask the children to identify a part of nature and have the group think about the different things that could be dependent on that object or that the object could depend upon. For example: One child suggests a tree. The group could guess that birds are dependent on the tree to build their nests, the tree is dependent on the earth to help it grow, the earth is dependent on rain to make it fertile, etc. Draw a picture that shows objects depending on each other.

SHOW NUMBER 105

Summary

Guest Readers

Mark Ritts

Tatiana Ali

Shari Belafonte

Zachary Bryan

Kino plays with a little red car and remembers when he went for a ride with Mark, who stopped to read him a book about driving in a red car. Zachary wants to read Kino one of his favorite books, but he can't find it. He goes to look for it, just missing Tatiana, who has found it. Kino is impatient for a story so Tatiana reads a book about a magic penny before going out to find Zachary. She talks with the children about what they would wish for. Shari reads a book about a magic house before she goes out to look for Tatiana and Zachary. They return without Shari, and then Kino gets to hear Zachary read his book about a Monster Mama.

BOOKS READ

My Little Red Car by Chris L. Demarest: A little boy dreams of traveling around the world in his little red car. He'll climb mountains, cross rivers, zip through cities and tunnels, visit the desert and the North Pole. When it gets dark, he'll head back home to sleep with his little red car. (themes: adventure, nature)

Three Wishes by Lucille Clifton, illustrated by Michael Hays: On New Year's Day, Zenobia finds a penny with her birth year on it while playing with her friend Victorius. That means she can make three wishes. After making two mistakes, she uses her third wish more wisely. (themes: friendship, fantasy, feelings [anger])

The Magic House by Robyn H. Eversole, illustrated by Peter Palagonia: April and her family live in a magic house full of special things — like a waterfall on the stairs. Her older sister Meredith doesn't believe in the magic, and when she comes near, the magic things disappear. One day Meredith is having a hard time practicing her swan dance for ballet. April leads her to her magic lake at the foot of the stairs, where Meredith practices and practices. Soon she starts looking more and more like a swan. (themes: family [siblings], imagination)

Monster Mama by Liz Rosenberg, illustrated by Stephen Gammell: Patrick Edward's mother is a monster, so she doesn't come out to be seen very much. He goes out to make friends on his own. One day, while out getting some strawberry dessert, Patrick Edward is harassed by a gang of boys who eat his dessert. He tries to cast a spell, but it doesn't work so he roars. His mother arrives and orders the boys home to make a new dessert. She assures Patrick Edward that she will always be there for him because she loves him. The boys return to Patrick Edward's house, and they all share the dessert. (themes: family [mother], feelings [love, teasing], sharing)

STORYPICKS

The Secret in the Matchbox by Val Willis, pictures by John Shelley

The Woman Who Flummoxed the Fairies
retold by Heather Forest, illustrated by Susan Gaber

ACTIVITIES

Game
Place two regular pennies and one "magic" penny in a cloth bag. Sit in a circle and take turns picking a penny. Someone who chooses the magic penny can tell the group what his or her three wishes would be. Anyone who gets a regular penny passes the bag to the next person. The game is played until every person has had a chance to say three wishes. Remind players to return the penny to the bag each time.

Crafts
Ask each child to choose a part of a house that they like, such as a porch, a brother's bedroom, steps, a closet, etc. Children will then use their imagination to draw magic versions of those parts of the house. When each child is finished, he or she will show and explain his or her drawing to the rest of the group. You can also "attach" the sections to create a house together.

Outside
Talk together about what you all would be doing if the weather were the opposite of what it is that day. You can also discuss what kinds of behavior and activities are only appropriate during certain times of the year (winter, Thanksgiving, etc.).

Summary

Guest Readers

Dave Coulier

Mariel Hemingway

Kino is disguised as a secret agent today. Lucy seems to be fooled, but she asks the secret agent why he looks so much like Kino. They decide to go ahead without Kino, and Dave reads the story of the gingerbread man. Afterward, Kino tries to fool Mariel, but she recognizes him. She reads the story of a cricket who learns to make his own sound, and then another book, one about a little boy who learns to whistle.

BOOKS READ

The Gingerbread Man by Eric A. Kimmel, illustrated by Megan Lloyd: An old couple make a gingerbread man, and just as they finish decorating him, he comes to life. He hops to the floor and runs out the door. The couple start running after him and are joined along the way by a sow, a dog, and a horse, who all try to stop him. When the gingerbread man gets to a river, a fox offers to carry him across. The gingerbread man rides on the fox's back until he is tricked into climbing onto the fox's snout and is eaten up. (themes: fairy tale, resourcefulness)

The Very Quiet Cricket by Eric Carle: From a tiny egg on a leaf, a cricket is born. He is greeted by the other insects but he cannot respond with a noise of his own. He rubs his wings together again and again, but each time there is no sound. Finally, he meets another cricket, rubs his wings together and a sound comes out. (themes: determination, sounds, nature, identity)**

Whistle for Willie by Ezra Jack Keats: Peter wishes he could whistle to his dog, Willie, but he does not know how. He plays around his house and his neighborhood, trying and practicing to blow. Finally, while hiding in a box, Peter succeeds and Willie comes running. (themes: determination, self-esteem, sounds)**

STORYPICKS

Who Killed Cock Robin? by Kevin O'Malley

Miss Rumphius story and pictures by Barbara Cooney

ACTIVITIES

Game
Use the masks (described in the crafts activity below) and any clothing items handy to play an identification game. Out of the view of the others, people will "transform" themselves. It will then be up to the others to determine the identity of those disguised.

Crafts
Give each child a piece of heavy paper about the size of his or her face, with holes cut out for the eyes, mouth, and nose. The child will then turn the mask into a disguise. After the disguise is complete, tie a piece of yarn to either side so that the mask may be worn. Write the child's name inside the mask.

Outside
Play a variation of hide-and-seek with noises. The person seeking will wear a blindfold, will be accompanied by an adult, and will attempt to find the other kids who are hiding. The children who are hiding must make noises such as whistles, claps, etc.

SHOW NUMBER 107

Summary

Guest Readers

Hector Elizondo

Kino's backpack is so full of his favorite toys that it is weighing him down. Mara reads him a story about a mouse whose house is too full, just like his backpack. Then she reads about a boy who takes long, funny walks with his mother. Afterward, she backs out of the Storyplace, like the boy in the book, and runs into Hector, who has come to read some books. He reads a story about a gentle bull and another about a young boy who helps an older friend.

BOOKS READ

Mouse's Birthday by Jane Yolen, illustrated by Bruce Degen: It is Mouse's birthday, but his house is very small. One by one the animals squeeze their way in with their presents. Then Mouse blows out his candles, which blows the house apart. The whole barn becomes his new house, and there is plenty of room for everyone. (themes: friendship, rhyme, size)

Jonathan and His Mommy by Irene Smalls-Hector, illustrated by Michael Hays: Jonathan loves to take walks with his Mommy. Together they take big steps, little steps, side steps, and scissors steps all across the neighborhood. (themes: family [mother], identity)**

The Story of Ferdinand by Munro Leaf, illustrated by Robert Lawson: Ferdinand is a gentle little bull who likes to sit under a cork tree and smell the flowers instead of butting and kicking like the others. One day five men come to pick out the fiercest and wildest bull for the bullfights in Madrid. Because Ferdinand accidentally sits on a bee and jumps and howls in pain, he is selected by the men and taken to Madrid in a cart. When the day of the bullfight arrives, the matadors and picadors are ready, but Ferdinand just sits in the center of the ring, quietly smelling the flowers. His career as a fighting bull is over, and he is carted back to his cork tree. (themes: uniqueness, animals)

Wilfrid Gordon McDonald Partridge by Mem Fox, illustrated by Julie Vivas: Wilfrid Gordon McDonald Partridge is a little boy who lives near a rest home. He has many friends there, but his favorite is Miss Nancy. When he learns from his parents that Miss Nancy is losing her memory, he starts asking the others what a memory is. He sets about collecting objects that represent the definitions they give and presents them to Miss Nancy. Each object rekindles an old memory for her, and in this way her memory is restored. (themes: friendship, caring/concern for others, feelings [generosity])

STORYPICKS

Owl Moon by Jane Yolen, illustrated by John Schoenherr

Grandfather's Journey by Allen Say

ACTIVITIES

Game
Players pick different small spaces in a room and see, for each space, how many people can fit in.

Crafts
Ask the children if they have seen a "cork" tree. Have them brainstorm other "silly" things to substitute for leaves. Collect these items and have children make their own make-believe trees. You can use buttons, bottle tops, pegs, etc., for leaves. Children can draw Ferdinand by the tree.

Outside
Take a walk like Jonathan and his mom, a variation on "Follow the Leader." Try taking all different kinds of steps — big, little, scissors, jumping, hopping, etc. Give each person a turn to lead the group.

SHOW NUMBER 108

Summary

Kino is feeling a little sad. He is staying with his aunt while his parents are away, but he thinks he's too old to miss his parents. Lucy assures him that you're never too old to miss the ones you love. Elena overhears them and offers to help by reading a book about three little owls who miss their mother. Kellie comes in and suggests that Kino needs a second set of parents. She reads a book about a couple who find a magic way to have two of everything. Afterward, everyone agrees that it is important to have someone special, and Patricia reads a book about a bird who doesn't have a mother and tries to find one.

Guest Readers

Kellie Williams

Lucy

Patricia Richardson

BOOKS READ

Owl Babies by Martin Waddell, illustrated by Patrick Benson: Three little owls are left alone one night to comfort each other while their mother is gone. Just as they start to imagine the worst, she arrives home to their nest. (themes: family [mother], feelings [sadness, comfort, fear])

Two of Everything by Lily Toy Hong: An old and poor couple dig up an old pot in their garden and learn that when you drop something in, two identical objects come out. They become richer and richer as they double the coins they throw in until, one day, the wife is knocked inside the pot. When her double is pulled out, the wife is furious, and as she fights with her husband, he accidentally falls in, too. Now the extra wife has an extra husband, and the two couples are able to live peacefully side by side. (themes: fairy tale, problem-solving)

A Mother for Choco by Keiko Kasza: A lonely little bird without a mother sets out to find one. After asking the giraffe, the penguin, and the walrus, Choco is in tears and ready to give up his search. Mrs. Bear comforts Choco and suggests that, although she doesn't look like him, perhaps she could be his mother. They head home, where Mrs. Bear's other children, a pig, a hippo, and an alligator, are waiting. (themes: family [mother], differences, feelings [comfort], animals)

STORYPICKS

This Quiet Lady by Charlotte Zolotow, pictures by Anita Lobel

On Mother's Lap by Ann Herbert Scott, illustrated by Glo Coalson

ACTIVITIES

Game
Fill a hat with miniatures or pictures of various things such as animals, people, or even places like a farm, a school, or a store. Each player will have a chance to pull an object and imagine what that object might miss.

Crafts
Ask the children to draw different parts of a face. Make sure that all parts are represented, and then let the kids mix and match to create a wide variety of faces with different features.

Outside
Role-play being doubles. Walk, run, or climb in unison. Also try the "mirror" exercise with each other. Facing each other, one child does something, and the second child copies what the first child did.

SHOW NUMBER 109

Summary

Guest Readers

Madge Sinclair

Kino talks about how his little sister has to go to school for the first time, and she's very nervous. Mara reads a book about a first day at school, then Madge and her granddaughter come in to read a book about a little girl who learns that she can be anything she wants to be. After a discussion about school, they move on to fairy tales and read Rumpelstiltskin. Finally, there is a visit with Lucy, who reads a book about a mom who is excellent.

B-18

BOOKS READ

Timothy Goes to School by Rosemary Wells: Timothy is starting a new school, but it seems that every day he shows up wearing the wrong thing. His mother keeps making him wear the "wrong" clothes, and Claude, who is always dressed just right, makes fun of him. Timothy doesn't want to go back to school at all until the day he meets Violet, who is also jealous of a little girl who seems to do everything right. (themes: friendship, feelings [jealousy, teasing])

Amazing Grace by Mary Hoffman, pictures by Caroline Binch: Grace loves to act out stories. When the teacher announces that the class will be performing Peter Pan, she is very excited. But then the kids in her class tell her she can't be Peter Pan because Peter isn't a girl, and he isn't black. When she reports this to her mother and Nana, they tell her she can be anything she wants. Nana takes her to the ballet to see an African American friend dance the role of Juliet. Grace is inspired to practice hard for the auditions and is unanimously voted the best for the role of Peter Pan. Her Nana reminds her that she can be anything she wants to be. (themes: uniqueness, differences, self-esteem)

Rumpelstiltskin retold and illustrated by Paul O. Zelinsky: A poor miller trying to impress the young king brags that his daughter can weave straw into gold. With the help of a little man who takes things in exchange for spinning straw into gold, the girl impresses the king so much that he marries her. Over time, the girl forgets that she has promised her firstborn child to the little man. When her son is born, she is challenged to guess the little man's name or give up her child. Luckily, a servant overhears the little man's name in the woods, tells the queen and the baby is saved. (themes: fairy tale, resourcefulness)

My Mom Is Excellent by Nick Butterworth: A little boy tells about all the different ways that his mother is excellent. (theme: family [mother])**

STORYPICKS

Koala Lou by Mem Fox, illustrated by Pamela Lofts

Mr. Rabbit and the Lovely Present by Charlotte Zolotow, pictures by Maurice Sendak

ACTIVITIES

Game
Ask each person to make up a silly name for something in the room. As a group, pick one "silly name" to use for something for the rest of the day or week. Label the silly name on the object.

Crafts
Ask children to draw a picture or write a letter to someone in their family who they think is "excellent," telling that person why.

Outside
Take a walk and notice the different jobs people do. (Children can also get ideas from books and magazines, if needed.) When you get back, draw or gather pictures of different people doing different things. Make a bulletin board of all the different jobs people can do.

SHOW NUMBER 110

Summary

Guest Readers

Telma Hopkins

Rene Auberjonois

Kino is practicing for the big spelling bee at school. He knows he will do well because he likes stories so much. To help him relax, Mara reads him a story about animals discovering a flower in the snow. They read a postcard from Desmond, who is riding on a plane with Telma, who reads him a book about a little girl and her cricket. When they return to Storytime, Kino has come in second place in the spelling bee because of a little mistake. To cheer him up, Rene reads about a cuddly penguin who wants to be left alone.

BOOKS READ

The Happy Day by Ruth Krauss, illustrated by Marc Simont: Snow is falling while the animals are sleeping. Gradually the animals wake up, sniff around them, and run together to a place in the snow where they find a single yellow flower, the only sign of color in a black-and-white winter. (themes: animals, nature, colors)**

Maggie and the Pirate by Ezra Jack Keats: Maggie has a pet cricket named Nicki that she keeps in a cage made by her father. One day, they are stolen by someone claiming to be a pirate. When Maggie finds the thief, the cricket is drowned in a struggle for the cage. Then the pirate, who turns out to be a new kid, comes with a new cricket in Nicki's cage. All the pirate wanted was the cage, because his own father never makes him anything. (themes: friendship, feelings)

Cuddly Dudley by Jez Alborough: Dudley the penguin loves to play alone, but his siblings love to huddle and cuddle with him. He escapes to a little house where he can be by himself. When his brothers and sisters and the owner of the house come after him, he runs away. But then Dudley gets lost. He follows the moon to the top of the hill and sees his siblings below. He is so happy to see them he waddles all the way down the hill for a big cuddle huddle. (themes: family, adventure)

STORYPICKS

The Snowy Day by Ezra Jack Keats

Choo Choo by Virginia Lee Burton

ACTIVITIES

Game
Hide a tape recorder that is playing the sound of a cricket. Have the group work together to locate the cricket.

Crafts
Give the children blank papers that are the size of postcards. They can then draw a faraway place on one side and write or dictate a small message on the other side of their postcards.

Outside
Take a walk and look for different colored things. As the leader, you can tell the children to point out red things, green things, etc.

B-21

SHOW NUMBER 111

Summary

Guest Readers

Alfre Woodard

Gordon Jump

Kino is busy collecting items for the recycling drive to raise money for library books. He even finishes Mara's drink so that he can have her can. He has time for a storybook visit with Alfre, who reads a book about a boy's adventure. Back at the Storyplace, Gordon calls him over to read a book about an elephant who keeps a promise. Kino points out that he is keeping a promise too by collecting for the recycling drive. Lucy promises to help him.

B-22

BOOKS READ

That's Good! That's Bad! by Margery Cuyler, illustrated by David Catrow: A little boy visiting the zoo with his parents gets carried up in the sky by his balloon. It carries him to the jungle through a series of accidents and near misses, where things that seem bad are actually good and things that seem good only lead to more bad. Finally, he is snatched up by a stork who carries him back to the zoo. (themes: fantasy, adventure, sequence of events)

Horton Hatches the Egg by Dr. Seuss: Maisey the lazy bird is tired of sitting on her egg and asks Horton the faithful elephant to help. Horton gets bored and tired but weathers out the seasons, tolerates the teasing of his friends, and puts up with his sale to the circus to protect the egg — because he promised Maisey that's what he would do. When Maisey happens to fly by the circus, and the egg is finally hatched, she decides she wants it back. But inside the egg is an elephant with wings. The crowd cheers for Horton and his baby, and he is sent home with his new charge. (themes: animals, responsibility, caring/concern for others)

STORYPICKS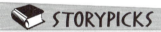

The Rainbabies by Laura Krauss Melmed

Ragtime Tumpie by Alan Schroeder, paintings by Bernie Fuchs

ACTIVITIES

Game
Have the players sit in a circle and all close their eyes. Hide an egg behind one person. After they all check behind them to see who has the egg, the person who has "laid" the egg now gets to hide it, until everybody has a turn. Try playing music to accompany the game.

Crafts
Encourage each child to draw an animal that lives in the jungle. Paste each animal onto poster board to make a jungle. As a group, children can draw in trees, the sun, and other jungle items. You could also use an old bedsheet and draw the jungle and animals on it with markers. (Hospitals often give away old bedsheets.)

Outside
Form a large circle and ask the children to think quietly about good and bad behaviors. Then go around the circle and have each child name a behavior. The group should respond by saying "That's good" or "That's bad." (You can also point out that some things are good in some places and bad in others — for example, it may be fine to use chalk on the cement at school but not outside a store.)

SHOW NUMBER 112

Summary

Kino is tired from doing chores for his mother. Mara reads him a book about a boy who also ends up with a series of jobs to do around the house. When Kino asks for another story, Christopher comes in to sing a song about a spider and tell a joke about a fly. He reads a book about insects at a formal party, and there is a picture book visit to Carl's house, where Carl and his family read a book about a rooster and a new chick.

Guest Readers

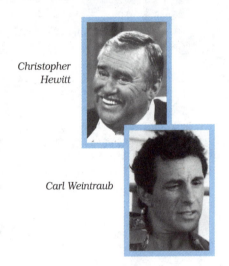

Christopher Hewitt

Carl Weintraub

BOOKS READ

If You Give a Mouse a Cookie by Laura Joffe Numeroff, illustrated by Felicia Bond: A mouse arrives at a boy's house and asks him for a cookie. When this request is granted, a new one is made, and the boy is led all over the house through a series of chores for his visitor. (theme: sequence of events)

Lady Bugatti by Joyce Maxner, illustrated by Kevin Hawkes: In a vividly illustrated book, a ladybug hosts a very formal dinner party for a few of her closest insect friends. Afterward, she takes them to a show, at the end of which she appears to give the prize to the best performance, by the owl. (themes: friendship, animals, vocabulary)

Little Peep by Jack Kent: An arrogant cock controls the farmyard and intimidates the other animals, who all believe that the sun comes up because the rooster crows. They warn Little Peep, who has just hatched, to stay out of the rooster's way. One night when Little Peep tries out a crow of his own, the farmer turns on the light, and all the animals are confused. The sun came up without the rooster! Little Peep admits that the sun came up because of his attempt to crow. The farmer turns off the light again, and Little Peep and the rooster argue through the night about who made the sun come up. They are so busy arguing that the sun comes up all by itself. They are both humbled, and peace is restored to the farmyard. (themes: self-esteem, animals, cause and effect)

STORYPICKS

The Very Quiet Cricket by Eric Carle

Strega Nona retold and illustrated by Tomie dePaola

ACTIVITIES

Game
In a circle, go around and have each person say what his or her favorite kind of cookie is. Then make a graph that shows how many people like each different kind of cookie.

Crafts
As a group, using a flip chart or poster board, write down a recipe for cookies that you will make. (You could choose to make the kind that most people like from the graph.) You can use a symbol or picture next to the words so that children who cannot read can still understand what each ingredient is. Then bake the cookies. Pre-measure the ingredients so that each child can add one item and have a turn to mix. The cookies could be eaten as a snack or brought home as a gift for family members.

Outside
Try a variation on tag where the person who is "it" is a rooster. A new person who is tagged must crow like a rooster to signify to the others that he or she is "it."

Summary

Guest Readers

A Martinez

Kino and Lucy are on the dock at the beach, painting pictures of the ocean. Lucy reads about a fish who can make wishes that come true. When Kino wishes for another story, they head back to the story corner where Mara is waiting to read them a story about a frog. Then A comes for a visit with his daughter and reads a book about a magic spring and another story about a little girl who visits her grandfather at the seaside. This reminds Kino about the painting he made, which Lucy has framed for him. A admires it so much that Kino tells him to keep it.

📚 BOOKS READ

The Fish Who Could Wish by John Bush, illustrated by Korky Paul: A fish with the ability to wish for anything he wants wishes that he could be like all the other fish, thus losing his unique gift. (themes: self-esteem, uniqueness)

Green Wilma by Tedd Arnold: One day Wilma wakes up green, lets out a croak and chases a buzzing fly. She seems to have turned into a frog. She hops into class, excels at dodge ball, inspires the other kids to paint themselves green in art class, and chases a fly out the door. Then she wakes up and remembers the lesson for all young frogs — that while you dream, you must never fall off a log. (themes: fantasy, identity)

Magic Spring by Nami Rhee: An old man and his wife are forced to work hard and alone because they have no child. After sipping from a magic spring, they are filled with new energy and become young again. Their neighbor wants to know how the couple became so young and handsome again and rushes off to drink from the magic spring. Being greedy, he takes more than one sip and he grows younger and younger, ending up as a baby. The couple arrive too late to save him but rejoice that they now can have the baby they always wanted. (themes: fairy tale, feelings [greed])

Stina by Lena Anderson: Every summer Stina visits her grandfather by the sea, where they go fishing and hunting for treasure. One night there is a terrible storm, and Stina's grandfather finds her crying outside in the rain. He gives her a hug and tells her the right way to watch a storm — you should always be with someone when you go out, and you should be properly dressed. They head out to watch, and Stina finds a present from the storm. (themes: family [grandfather], feelings [curiosity, fear], nature)

📚 STORYPICKS

The Great Adventure of Wo Ti by Nathan Zimelman, illustrated by Julie Downing

Stina's Visit by Lena Anderson

ACTIVITIES

Game
Create a simple treasure hunt where the group works together to find items from clues you have given them. The final treasure will be a drinking spot where they can each have a "magic sip."

Crafts
From big pieces of paper, cut out frames big enough to frame an 8.5" x 11" piece of paper. The kids can decorate the frames with markers or paint or by gluing gold and silver glitter for a fancy effect. Use the frame for art the children have created.

Outside
Ask the children to play around as if they were frogs, just like Wilma in the story. They could also play leapfrog.

Storytime

SHOW NUMBER 114

Summary

Kino is tired. He has entered a contest at school where he must read ten books in ten days. He forgot that today is the last day, and he has only read seven. Mara offers to help him out and gives him a book to read aloud about a boy who is having a problem with his eyes. Then Jeff comes in to read a book about a turtle who is afraid of the inside of his small, dark shell. For the tenth book, they go on a picture book visit to a garden with Wes, who reads a Native American Cinderella story.

Guest Readers

Jeff Altman

Mara

BOOKS READ

The Boy with Square Eyes by Juliet and Charles Snape: Charlie watches television so much that his eyes become square, and everything he looks at appears to be square. The doctor suggests that Charlie exercise his eyes. Charlie and his mother go to an art gallery, to the library, and to the park. At home, they unplug the television, and Charlie draws a picture, does a puzzle, reads a book, and looks out his window. As he starts to wonder "Why?," his eyes become round again, and he never sees things again in quite the same way. (themes: uniqueness [perspective], problem-solving)

Franklin in the Dark by Paulette Bourgeois, illustrated by Brenda Clark: A young turtle is afraid of small, dark places, so he sets out to get help, dragging his shell behind him. He meets a series of animals who are also afraid of things in their lives — a duck afraid of deep water, a lion afraid of loud noises, a polar bear afraid of cold nights. They each have a special way to handle their fears, and, inspired by them, Franklin learns to use a night-light before he goes to sleep in his shell. (themes: feelings [fear], differences, problem-solving, resourcefulness)

The Rough-Face Girl by Rafe Martin, illustrated by David Shannon: In this Native American version of the Cinderella story, a poor man lives in a village with his three daughters. The two oldest daughters are cruel to their younger sister, who has become ugly and scarred from her work at their fire and is known as the Rough-Face Girl. They all dream of marrying The Invisible Being, who lives with his sister in a large, beautiful wigwam. The legend is that only the girl who can truly see The Invisible Being can marry him. The cruel sisters try but fail to recognize him. Only the humble Rough-Face Girl can truly see the signs of him in the beauty of nature around her. (themes: fairy tale, identity)

STORYPICKS

Little Toot by Hardie Gramatky

The Butterfly Jar poems by Jeff Moss, illustrated by Chris Demarest

ACTIVITIES

Game
Ask the group to come up with a list of different kinds of people (e.g., little boy, big girl, firefighter, doctor) and write down their suggestions. Divide the group into two straight lines. The person at the head of one line must come up with a "fear" that someone from the list might have. The person from the second line must come up with a "solution" to this fear. Switch so that all participants have a chance to come up with a fear and a solution.

Crafts
Make glasses using stiff construction paper. Using a pattern, cut the glass frames out of paper and glue circles of tinted cellophane to the inside of the frames. Have the children try them on and see how different things look through different colors. (Note: You can purchase colored cellophane at arts and crafts or teacher supply stores.)

Outside
Assign a different color or shape to each child. Encourage the children to look around outside and list or draw all the things they found that had their color or shape.

SHOW NUMBER 115

Summary

Kino is putting on a magic show and is dressed as a magician. As a first trick, Kathy reads a story about a magic bed. Kino then asks her for her opinion on a new book about monsters, which she asks him to read. Afterward, he makes Mara and Kathy disappear. Then Lucy and Arte come to read another book, one about a magic bone.

Guest Readers

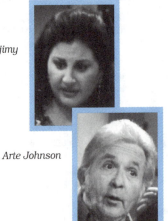

Kathy Najimy

Arte Johnson

B-30

BOOKS READ

Two Badd Babies by Jeffie R. Gordon, illustrated by Chris L. Demarest: Two babies are put down for their nap, but they're not tired. They rock and bounce their crib so much it rolls them all over town. They stop at a bakery for pastry, go to the movies, have a hamburger, stop by their father's bookstore and then, finally tired, head back home for their nap. (themes: fantasy, adventure)

Go Away, Big Green Monster! by Ed Emberley: This is a color cut-out book of different colors and shapes that accumulate to create a big green monster and then slowly come apart to make him disappear. (themes: feelings [fear], shapes, colors)**

The Amazing Bone by William Steig: One day while dawdling home, Pearl the pig finds a bone that can make many noises. It manages to scare off robbers who try to steal her purse. Unfortunately, it is not able to scare off a fox who is planning to eat Pearl. The fox is about to cook Pearl when the bone chants nonsense words that make him shrink to nothing. Pearl returns home with her bone, which becomes a member of her family. (themes: fantasy, feelings [fear])

STORYPICKS

Big Al by Andrew Clements, illustrated by Yoshi

Thunder Cake by Patricia Polacco

ACTIVITIES

Game
Give each person two colored shapes. The players will take turns pasting one shape at a time onto a big poster board until they have collectively created a monster. Then remove the shapes to make the monster disappear.

Crafts
The children can draw the babies from *Two Badd Babies* in various places around town. After the drawings are complete, they can write or dictate a few lines about what the babies are doing and how the people are reacting to them.

Outside
Play a "Pearl the pig" game. One child will be Pearl, another one the talking bone, and the others can act as the people who encounter this odd sight.

Summary

Guest Readers

Mario Lopez

Cindy Williams

Kino is very excited — his mother said he could have a slumber party, though he's not quite sure what that is. The kids come in to read a book, and he invites them all to sleep over. Lucy reads a book about getting dressed, and the kids participate by miming the dressing that goes on in the book. At the slumber party, Mario reads a spooky ghost story. Back at the Storyplace, Cindy reads a book about a bunny who does not know what he is.

 ## BOOKS READ

Froggy Gets Dressed by Jonathan London, illustrated by Frank Remkiewicz: When Froggy wakes up to find snow outside, he is eager to get out and play. He's on his way out the door when his mother tells him he forgot his pants. He repeatedly gets dressed and undressed as his mother each time reminds him of an article of clothing he has forgotten to put on. (themes: family [mother], responsibility)

Ghost's Hour, Spook's Hour by Eve Bunting, illustrated by Donald Carrick: A little boy and his dog wake up in the middle of the night and explore the scary noises all over the house. After finding the causes of each noise, they curl up with the boy's parents, whom they find sleeping in the living room. (themes: feelings [fear, courage], sounds)

Daley B by Jon Blake, illustrated by Axel Scheffler: Daley B, the bunny, does not know what kind of animal he is, and he wonders why his feet are so big. One day the other bunnies warn him that Jazzy D the weasel is coming — and he loves to eat rabbits. All the rabbits escape except Daley B. Suddenly, he realizes that he is a rabbit and uses his big feet to jump so hard that the weasel is sent back to where he came from. (themes: identity, problem-solving)

STORYPICKS

Martha Speaks by Susan Meddaugh

Time for Bed by Mem Fox, illustrated by Jane Dyer

ACTIVITIES

Game

Tape record various noises in the room. Play the noises one at a time, and have the group work together to figure out what each noise is. For example, it could be a door shutting, two blocks hitting each other, the sink running — sounds they hear during the course of a normal day but may not think about as individual sounds.

Crafts

Fold an 8.5" x 11" piece of paper in half. Ask the children to draw one picture of themselves on each half with totally different clothes on each side. For example, at home vs. at a wedding, in winter vs. summer, etc.

Outside

Play the mime dressing game. Each child will have a turn to face the group and pretend to be doing an everyday activity such as brushing his or her teeth or getting dressed. The others will attempt to mimic the activities and movements of the "leader."

SHOW NUMBER 117

Summary

Guest Readers

Belita Moreno

Ronn Lucas

Maria Conchita Alonso

Kino has a new library card and is eager to share his new book, which is about a mom who is a witch. Afterward, they are joined by Ronn and his dragon puppet, Scorch, who reads a book about a family and their dragon. Then there is a picture book visit with Maria who reads a story in another place to get books — a bookstore.

BOOKS READ

The Trouble with Mom by Babette Cole: Mom is not like most moms — she wears funny hats, rides along on a broomstick, and doesn't get along with the other parents at school, whom she turns into frogs. The kids at school love playing at Mom's haunted house, but the other parents refuse to let their children play there anymore — Mom is too different. One day, the school catches fire, and Mom arrives on a broomstick, causes a rainstorm, and puts the fire out. Now the children are allowed to play at her house once again. (themes: family [mother], differences)

The Dragon of an Ordinary Family by Margaret Mahy, illustrated by Helen Oxenbury: The Belsacki family is a very ordinary family whose life is turned upside down when Mr. Belsacki brings home a small dragon as a pet. The dragon grows to be so big and so unordinary that their neighbors and friends stop coming. The dragon moves on, and the family follows him to the Isle of Magic for their vacation. Afterward, they fly home on a magic carpet with a more ordinary pet — a kitten. But when they get home, the kitten opens its mouth to speak. (themes: fantasy, family)

Borreguita and the Coyote translated and retold by Verna Aardema, illustrated by Petra Mathers: Living at the foot of a mountain, Borreguita is a little lamb whom a wolf wants to eat for dinner. Using different tricks, she is able to stop him from eating her. Finally, when he threatens to eat her immediately, she asks him to swallow her whole. He opens his mouth, she charges for it, and his mouth is so hurt that he runs away and never comes back. (themes: fairy tale, resourcefulness)

STORYPICKS

The Amazing Bone by William Steig

Silent Lotus by Jeanne M. Lee

ACTIVITIES

Game

In *The Trouble With Mom*, the mother turns other parents into frogs. Play a game based on this idea in which one person stands in front of the others and tells them all to act like a certain animal. Give each person a turn to be the leader.

Crafts

Give each child same-shaped pieces of paper in different sizes, ranging from a business card size up to 8.5" x 11" or even bigger. Ask the children each to draw the dragon at a different stage of its growth. When they are finished, arrange the pictures in order of size. Note: Bigger pieces are not "better"; every piece is necessary for the final result.

Outside

Visit the library. At the library, the children who do not have library cards can apply for their own cards and each check out a book. (You can check with the librarian ahead of time about availability of books on particular topics.) Note: You may need to call ahead to the library to check on age requirements and identification that will be needed from the kids. You may also need a parent's signature on a child's library card application.

SHOW NUMBER 118

Summary

Shari Lewis is visiting in the backyard with Lamb Chop and reads a story about an Appalachian family. The kids participate by repeating the title phrase about a possum. Back at the Storyplace, Paul comes to read a story about a colorful elephant and another about a little girl who goes on an adventure with her grandmother. Afterward, everyone talks about imagination. Finally, there is a picture book visit to Cloris's kitchen, where she reads a book about a hungry Thing to her grandchildren.

Guest Readers

Shari Lewis

Paul Rodriguez

Cloris Leachman

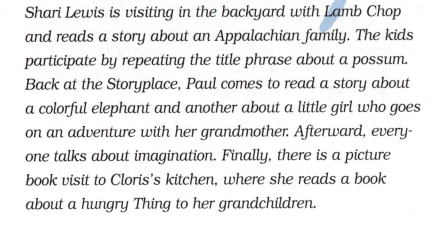

BOOKS READ

Possum Come A-Knockin' by Nancy Van Laan, illustrated by George Booth: The members of a large family are all busy doing their own things when a possum comes to knock on the door. When each finally hears the knocking and they all stop what they are doing, the narrator announces that a possum is at the door. But when Father opens the door, the possum is hiding. The whole family goes back to their noisy activities. (themes: family, sequence of events)

Elmer by David McKee: Elmer is a patchwork-colored elephant. Though he makes everyone laugh and keeps them happy, he doesn't like being different. He paints himself gray to be like the rest of the elephants, but then nobody laughs anymore. The rain washes away his paint. Elmer is fun again, and all the elephants celebrate Elmer Day by decorating themselves to look just like him. (themes: friendship, differences, colors, uniqueness)

Abuela by Arthur Dorros, illustrated by Elisa Kleven: Rosalba and her grandmother love to explore New York City together. One day they fly up into the sky like birds and explore the city from above. They pass over the busy city, travel to Abuela's native island, rest high up in the clouds, pass the windows of Papa's work, and land back in the park for a boat ride on the lake. (themes: family [grandmother], imagination, adventure)

The Hungry Thing by Jan Slepian and Ann Seidler, pictures by Richard E. Martin: One day a very hungry Thing arrives in town wearing a sign that says "Feed Me." Unfortunately, no one can understand what foods he is asking for. Finally a little boy realizes that schmancakes is pancakes and tickles is pickles. They offer the Thing many different foods, mispronouncing them all until at last he turns the sign around. He is full. (themes: rhyme, caring/concern for others, problem-solving)

STORYPICKS

Miss Nelson Is Missing by Harry Allard, illustrated by James Marshall

Sleeping Ugly by Jane Yolen, pictures by Diane Stanley

ACTIVITIES

Game
Play a food mispronunciation game. On index cards or pieces of cardboard or paper, draw or paste pictures of kinds of food. Place all the cards in a hat or box. Each person will pick a card with a picture of a food on it. Then ask them to make up a name like schmancakes for pancakes or tickles for pickles.

Crafts
Ask the children to draw rainbow elephants. This can be done with paints, markers, watercolors or crayons. Post the drawings for all to admire the colorful herd.

Outside
Find a place to sit outside and look up at clouds. Ask children, just like Rosalba and her Abuela, to use their imaginations to identify what the clouds look like — a bird, an island, a boat, a building, etc. Ask the children to draw pictures of what the clouds looked like to them.

SHOW NUMBER 119

Summary

Guest Readers

Ellen DeGeneres

Meshach Taylor

As Lucy paints, Kino admires her parrot, Pete, and his beautiful colors. She shows him how to make these colors by mixing her paints. Then she reads Kino a story about a witch who changes the colors of things around her. Afterward, Lucy asks Kino to watch Pete while she goes out for more seed. But Kino opens the door, and the parrot flies away. He is relieved to find that Pete has flown over to Mara and Ellen. Ellen reads a book about a lost parrot who learns his colors. Afterward, there is a picture book visit to the library with Meshach and his daughters, where they read a book about a little boy and his teddy bear and another about three sisters who do everything together.

B-38

📚 BOOKS READ

Winnie the Witch by Valerie Thomas, illustrated by Korky Paul: Winnie the Witch lives in a very black house. Unfortunately, this makes it hard to see Wilbur, her black cat. When she makes him green, she can't see him when he's outside in the grass. When she makes him multicolored, he is so embarrassed that he hides in a tree. Finally, Winnie turns him black again and colors everything else in her house. At last she can see Wilbur. (themes: imagination, colors, problem-solving)

The Last Time I Saw Harris by Frank Remkiewicz: Edmond has a parrot named Harris whom he teaches many things using flash cards. The only thing Harris hasn't learned yet is the color purple. One day a windstorm takes Harris away. Edmond sets out with his flash cards and his chauffeur to find the parrot. After traveling across the world, repairing dents on the car with colored parts (including a purple trunk), they are driving along under a tree when they hear Harris say "purple." They have found the lost parrot, and he has learned the color purple at last. (themes: friendship, adventure, colors)

Eddie and Teddy by Gus Clarke: Eddie and Teddy are always together until it is time for Eddie to start school. The friends are very sad to be apart, but gradually Eddie learns to like school and to make new friends. Teddy is so sad and lonely at home that Mother asks the teacher if Teddy can go to school. The teacher agrees and the old friends are happily reunited. (themes: friendship, feelings [sadness])

One of Three by Angela Johnson, illustrated by David Soman: Three sisters do everything together, but sometimes the youngest one is left out of things because she is too young. Soon she learns that she can be one of three when she is alone with her parents. This is a different kind of three but it's just as nice. (themes: family [siblings], feelings [being left out])

📚 STORYPICKS

Where's My Teddy? by Jez Alborough

A Job for Wittilda by Caralyn and Mark Buehner

ACTIVITIES

Game
Divide the group into pairs. Take turns presenting flash cards to each other. The cards could have colors, simple words, or animals on them. The person who is looking at the card has to guess what is on it. Each pair should have a turn at presenting and guessing.

Crafts
Ask children to draw a picture with things that are "hidden" inside. This can be done by making the subject very small, creating a busy background, or using similar colors.

Outside
Take a walk together around your neighborhood, and look for things that are purple. When you return from the walk, have everyone draw a picture of one of the purple things noticed in the neighborhood.

SHOW NUMBER 120

Summary

It is Kino's birthday, and Mara is planning a surprise for him. She recites a poem she wrote about how happy she is to have Storytime with him and reads him a story to help him remember the love he got as a baby. His friends come in for a story, and Kino opens his present, a stamp to personalize all of his books. Patricia Polacco joins them to read a book she wrote about a grandmother and her doll, a story based on her own Russian grandmother. As a final treat, there is a picture book visit with Reggie to a theater dressing room to read about a little girl and her grandfather.

Guest Readers

Mara

Reggie Vel Johnson

 **BOOKS READ**

More, More, More, Said the Baby by Vera B. Williams: This book shows different babies and the people who love them, tossing and hugging them, admiring their toes and bellies, and playing affectionately with them. (themes: family, differences)**

Babushka's Doll by Patricia Polacco: Natasha loves to visit her grandmother, her Babushka, on weekends, but she sometimes gets bored while the older woman goes about her daily chores. This makes her impatient, and she demands Babushka's attention "now." One day Babushka leaves Natasha to play with a special doll that comes to life and torments Natasha with impatient demands until the little girl bursts into tears. When Babushka returns, the doll becomes a doll again, and Natasha learns to be a more patient little girl. (themes: fantasy, responsibility)

Grandpa's Face by Eloise Greenfield, illustrated by Floyd Cooper: Tamika loves her grandfather, who is an actor. She especially loves his face, which tells her everything about him. But one day, while he is rehearsing, she sees a face she does not know. It is cold and hard and it makes her afraid. When she tells him about this face, he assures her that he was only practicing. He loves her, and she will never see that face directed at her. (themes: family [grandfather], feelings [fear, love])

STORYPICKS

The New Kid on the Block poems by Jack Prelutsky, drawings by James Stevenson

The Dog Who Had Kittens by Polly M. Robertus, illustrated by Janet Stevens

ACTIVITIES

Game
Place index cards with drawings of faces that express a variety of emotions (happy, sad, angry, frustrated, etc.) into a hat. Ask each participant to pick a card and act out the mood with his or her face. The others will guess what the emotion is. The cards are returned to the hat, and every person gets a turn.

Crafts
Use potatoes to make stamps. Cut large potatoes in half. Using a marker, the children can draw simple shapes onto the cut ends of the potatoes. An adult can then cut the shapes out so the children are ready to use their stamps. Make this into a literacy activity by having children label their shapes.

Outside
Using an oversized piece of lined paper, create a group poem about things found outside. Each child will offer one line that may or may not rhyme with the previous line.

SHOW NUMBER 121

Summary

Kino greets Lucy by reciting a rhyme. Lucy responds by reading him a rhyming book about a boy and a bear and the berries they love. Then Bill comes in to read a spooky book he wrote, which is also in rhyme. He and the kids talk about being scared. Afterward, there is a picture book visit with Edward, who reads a book about a baby rattlesnake who is a little too eager to be more grown up.

Guest Readers

Lucy

Edward James Olmos

B-42

 **BOOKS READ**

Jamberry by Bruce Degen: A boy and a bear recite in rhyme about different berries and how much they love them. (theme: rhyme)**

The Ghost-Eye Tree by Bill Martin, Jr. and John Archambault, illustrated by Ted Rand: One night a boy and his sister head out to buy milk for their mother. On the way they must pass the scary ghost-eye tree. The sister teases her brother for being frightened, but on the way home from their errand they are both frightened and run past the tree. When the sister discovers that her brother has lost his hat, she goes back to get it for him. (themes: family [siblings], feelings [fear, courage], adventure)

Baby Rattlesnake by Te Ata and Lynn Moroney, illustrated by Veg Reisberg: A baby rattlesnake is eager to have his own rattle, but his parents tell him he is too young. He begs and cries and keeps all the older rattlesnakes up until they decide to give in. They give him the rattle but warn him not to use it foolishly. Not listening, he shakes his rattle at the chief's daughter, who crushes it with her foot. His beautiful rattle is lost, but his family comforts him with hugs that make him feel better. (themes: family, responsibility, feelings [comfort])

 **STORYPICKS**

Never Spit on Your Shoes story and pictures by Denys Cazet

This Is the Hat by Nancy Van Laan, pictures by Holly Meade

ACTIVITIES

Game
Have everyone sit in a circle. Pick a person to say any word randomly. The player next to him or her will think of a rhyming word, and the game will continue until everybody has had at least one turn.

Crafts
Make snake "rattles" together. Glue together two paper plates that have been decorated by the children and filled with rice or a similar dry grain. Discuss where and when it is appropriate to use their new toys.

Outside
Ask each child to think about something he or she used to be afraid of but isn't any more. Discuss why the child is no longer afraid and what helped conquer this fear.

Summary

Mara has invited Alley to come and read a story about a family's special Christmas tree. Alley tells of one Christmas she spent on an island, where she decorated a palm tree. Kino suggests another book about a tree, which Alley remembers is about an old lady and a bird. Then Vicki reads another story about a new girl at school who is a little too eager to fit in.

Guest Readers

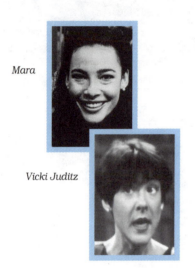

Mara

Vicki Juditz

 BOOKS READ

Night Tree by Eve Bunting, illustrated by Ted Rand: On the night before Christmas, a boy and his family set out on their annual ritual of decorating a special tree in a forest near their home. They cover the tree with natural goodies for the animals and gather underneath to admire its beauty and sing Christmas carols. (themes: holidays [Christmas], family, sharing, music, nature)

Maebelle's Suitcase by Tricia Tusa: Maebelle is 108 years old, loves birds, and lives in a tree house so she can be near her friends. She is putting the finishing touches on her entry for the local hat contest when her bird friend Binkle stops by to borrow a suitcase for his trip south for the winter. But the suitcase is too heavy for Binkle to fly with, so Maebelle pretends she needs the items inside to add to her hat, saving his pride and allowing him to fly south before it gets too cold. (themes: friendship, problem-solving)

Ruby, the Copy Cat by Peggy Rathmann: Ruby is the new girl at school, and she very much wants to fit in. She begins to copy everything that Angela, the girl in front of her, does and says. At first Angela likes this, but after a while she becomes annoyed and no longer wants to be Ruby's friend. Their teacher, Miss Hart, tries to encourage Ruby to be herself. When she shows the class her own talent in hopping, they realize that she is special, too. (themes: friendship, uniqueness)

STORYPICKS

Fly Away Home by Eve Bunting, illustrated by Ronald Himler

A Three Hat Day by Laura Geringer, pictures by Arnold Lobel

ACTIVITIES

Game
After doing the crafts activity below, have a hat contest. Each person can take a turn modeling his or her hat for the other people. Everyone should receive an award in the contest, i.e., brightest, bluest, silliest, funniest, etc.

Crafts
Show children how to make hats by affixing a piece of paper to a head-shaped band. The top part of the hat can be decorated in any way that the child wants. Look for items from the playground that can be incorporated into the hat, such as leaves or sticks. The children can write their names on the hats to identify them as their own.

Outside
Take a visit to the neighborhood or park to look at trees. Before leaving, you could talk about which kinds of trees you will be looking for, such as a tree that would or would not fit inside a house, a tree that has fruit or berries, a tree where an animal lives, a tree that looks like a Christmas tree, etc.

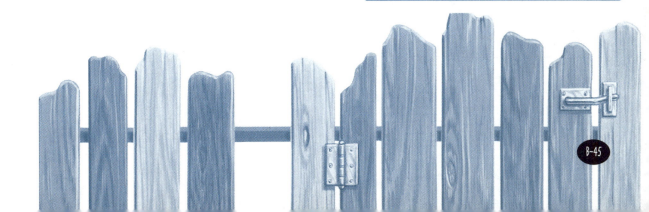

SHOW NUMBER 123

Summary

Kino is dressed like a chef today. He has brought in some chili he made with his father and has brought the makings of a great peanut butter sandwich. But when he opens his bag, he realizes he has forgotten half of the ingredients. Lucy teaches him to improvise by dipping a banana in his peanut butter. Then she reads a book about another kind of chef. Tamlyn comes in to read a book about a vain emperor and another about a duck who is confused about what he is.

Guest Readers

Tamlyn Tomita

 **BOOKS READ**

The Wolf's Chicken Stew by Keiko Kasza: A wolf who loves to cook and to eat finds a chicken for his stew. He decides to fatten her up by baking her delicious goodies, which he leaves on her stoop. When it is time to get the chicken for the stew, he is greeted by the baby chicks, who are grateful for his tasty gifts. His conscience intervenes, and he cannot eat the chickens, so he joins them for a dinner made by their mother. (themes: sharing, cause and effect)

The Emperor's New Clothes retold and illustrated by S.T. Mendelson: In this version of the classic tale about a vain emperor, the characters are animals. (themes: identity, feelings [vanity], fairy tale)

Duckat by Gaelyn Gordon, illustrated by Chris Gaskin: One day a duck arrives on Mabel's doorstep and says "meow." Mabel soon sees that the duck also acts like a cat — he hates the pond, loves milk, chases mice, and is scared up the lamppost by a dog. When Mabel tells him that if he is a cat, he won't be able to come down, the duck finally acts like a duck and flies. The next day a cat appears on Mabel's doorstep and says "quack." (themes: imagination, differences, animals, identity)

 **STORYPICKS**

Beware of Boys by Tony Blundell

The Day of Ahmed's Secret by Florence Parry Heide and Judith Heide Gilliland, illustrated by Ted Lewin

ACTIVITIES

Game
Let each person take a turn at talking like one animal while physically acting like another. The rest of the group can guess what the two animals are.

Crafts
Ask children to draw their favorite animal. Then cut each animal in half and have the children match different animal halves to make combination animals. They could also think of names for the "new" types of animals.

Outside
Visit a farmer's market or a supermarket. While looking at the different foods, ask the children to think about what different things do or do not go together.

SHOW NUMBER 124

Summary

Guest Readers

Rosana DeSoto

Kino has a surprise — his friend Rosana has come to read a story about a man who had the same dream three times, which leads him to a treasure. They talk about how the real treasures are here — friends and stories. Their next story is about a little mouse who is not so happy about her new baby brother. Bob comes in singing and reads a musical book about a band of hedgehogs. The kids have fun participating by making sounds with kazoos.

BOOKS READ

The Treasure by Uri Shulevitz: Isaac is a very poor old man who dreams three times that he must go to the capital city to look for a treasure under a bridge near the royal palace. He travels all the way there, only to be laughed at by the guards at the bridge. When Isaac explains why he is there, the captain of the guards laughs that he dreamt that he must look in a pot under the stove of a poor old man. Isaac travels all the way home, discovers the treasure under the stove in his home, and builds a house of prayer to give thanks. (themes: determination, feelings [hope], sharing)

Julius, the Baby of the World by Kevin Henkes: Lily is not happy. She has a new baby brother whom her parents adore and who she thinks is disgusting. She taunts him in his crib, tries to frighten him, and wishes he would go away. Then one day, at a party, one of her cousins also calls Julius disgusting. Lily is so furious she defends her baby brother. She admires him and kisses him and makes her cousin do the same. (themes: family [siblings], feelings [jealousy, love])

The Happy Hedgehog Band by Martin Waddell, illustrated by Jill Barton: Harry the hedgehog makes a drum. The other hedgehogs are so impressed that they make their own drums and form a band. The other animals in the forest admire the band and want to play too. Harry tells them to join in by contributing their own special noises to the band. (themes: friendship, resourcefulness, music)

STORYPICKS

The Story of Ferdinand by Munro Leaf, drawings by Robert Lawson

Flossie and the Fox by Patricia C. McKissack, pictures by Rachel Isadora

ACTIVITIES

Game

As in the book where the treasure was right under the stove, hide a small object in a familiar place. Encourage the players to ask questions about where the treasure is. You can respond by saying "You're getting hot" (if they are close to it), "cold" (if they are far away), or "warm" (if they are somewhat close to it). Each person should have a turn to ask a question about where the treasure is. Note: The "treasure" could be a picture of a special person who is coming to visit, a field trip you are planning to take, or a special treat you are planning to make together.

Crafts

Make musical instruments. You can recycle old yogurt containers by placing beans inside them, covering them, and using them as shakers. Personalize the containers by gluing decorations on the outside. Or decorate two paper plates, and glue them together with beans inside.

Outside

Create an orchestra. Ask each child to think of a sound to make by singing, clapping, snapping fingers, etc. In a large group, have one child make his or her sound; the next child then repeats the sound of the previous child and adds his or her own sound, and so on, until the last child has a turn.

SHOW NUMBER 125

Summary

Kino dreams about a trip he took to the beach, where Holly reads a book about a family's vacation at the beach. When he wakes up, Bill comes over to read a book about a dog with no friends. But Kino is sad because he woke up from his dream before going into the water. To cheer him up, Mara suggests that Bill read a funny book about a rooster.

Guest Readers

Mara

Bill Cobbs

 **BOOKS READ**

Greetings from Sandy Beach by Bob Graham: A family piles into their car for a vacation at the beach. With the help of a group of dangerous-looking bikers and an unruly crowd of school kids, they set up their tent, play in the water, and manage to have a good time. (themes: family, adventure, cooperation)

Socrates by Rascal and Gert Bogaerts: Socrates is an orphaned dog who lives alone on the streets. He dreams of having a friend. One day he finds a pair of glasses and puts them on. Everywhere he goes, he gets smiles. Finally he is making friends. Then he stops to listen to a musician, who is thrilled to find that Socrates has found his missing glasses. Now he can find his way home, and he takes Socrates in to live with him. (themes: friendship, sharing)

The Rooster Who Went to His Uncle's Wedding by Alma Flor Ada, illustrated by Kathleen Kuchera: The rooster is getting ready for his uncle's wedding when he stoops in the mud for a kernel of corn. When he asks for help cleaning his beak, he sets off a sequence of events involving the grass, a lamb, a dog, a stick, a campfire, a brook, and the sun. (themes: sequence of events, nature, animals, problem-solving)

STORYPICKS

Hattie and the Fox by Mem Fox, illustrated by Patricia Mullins

Me First by Helen Lester, illustrated by Lynn Munsinger

ACTIVITIES

Game
Ask everyone to think of something to bring to the beach or things to do at the beach. (If there is no beach in your area, use another summer destination.) Have them take turns pantomiming, so that the others can guess what it is. Then, compile a list of all the suggested ideas.

Crafts
Break the *Socrates* story down into sections, and assign one section to each child. Give each child a piece of paper on which to draw his or her part of the story. When all of the pictures are displayed together, it will be the children's version of the original book.

Outside
Take a trip to the beach or another summer destination. With the list the children have created in the game above, they will know exactly what to bring and will have some great ideas about what to do once there. Of course, this trip will require advance planning and chaperones to come along.

SHOW NUMBER 126

Summary

Kino has lost his roller blades and is very sad. To cheer him up, Barbara reads a book about telling a story. It's a good one, but he still feels sad, so she reads another about a misnamed porcupine. Finally, Markus comes in with Kino's roller blades, which were left at his house. Kino is so happy he asks Markus to read him another story about Christmas.

Guest Readers

Barbara Bain

Markus Redmond

 **BOOKS READ**

Aunt Isabel Tells a Good One by Kate Duke: Penelope the mouse asks her aunt to tell her a story. Together they make up a story about Lady Nell, who falls in love with Prince Augustus, whose parents don't approve. Then the prince is kidnapped by a mole and a bat. When Lady Nell rescues the prince from his cave, she is a heroine, and the two can live happily ever after. (themes: feelings, adventure)

A Porcupine Named Fluffy by Helen Lester, illustrated by Lynn Munsinger: A porcupine couple admire and adore their first child so much that they name him Fluffy. But Fluffy is embarrassed by a name that doesn't seem to fit and tries everything to make himself more fluffy, like his name. (themes: friendship, identity, self-esteem, feelings [embarrassment])

Morris's Disappearing Bag by Rosemary Wells: It's Christmas day, and Morris and his siblings are opening their presents. The older kids all get fancy new toys but Morris gets a bear that no one is interested in. Then he opens his last gift, a disappearing bag. When he gets inside, no one can see him. All the older kids want to try out the disappearing bag, and now they are willing to share their toys. (themes: family, sharing)

STORYPICKS

The Whingdingdilly written and illustrated by Bill Peet

Heckedy Peg by Audrey Wood, illustrated by Don Wood

ACTIVITIES

Game
Play a name game. Each person can say one name that he or she really likes or make up a name that rhymes with his or her real name. Participants can also say if they were named for a special person and why.

Crafts
Make porcupines together. This can be done with all-purpose clay and toothpicks. After the body has been formed, add toothpicks. Be sure that the children leave a place to hold on to their porcupines.

Outside
Take some old pillowcases or sacks to a grassy area and have a sack race. Afterward, each child can get inside the pillowcase or sack and tell the other children about a special place he or she is pretending to be in.

SHOW NUMBER 127

Summary

Kino sings "Old MacDonald Had a Farm," which makes Lucy think of a book about a farmer who is a duck. After she reads it, they talk about working on a farm and about animals who talk. Then Raven stops by to read a scary book that she got from the library. Lucy explains to Kino that dragons only exist in one's imagination. Jamie arrives to read a story about a fortune-teller, and Kino tries to read the future in a basketball.

Guest Readers

Raven-Symoné

Jamie Farr

B-54

 **BOOKS READ**

Farmer Duck by Martin Waddell, illustrated by Helen Oxenbury: A duck lives with a very lazy farmer and is forced to do all the work while the farmer lounges in bed. The poor duck is so exhausted and sad that the other animals decide to help him by tossing the farmer out of bed and chasing him off the farm. From then on, all the animals work together and share the responsibility of the farm. (theme: cooperation)

I Hear a Noise by Diane Goode: A little boy hears a noise. His mother tells him it's nothing, but suddenly a monster dragon swoops him up to the sky with the other monsters. When the dragon's mother learns what he has done, she orders him to take the little boy back home where he belongs. (themes: family [mother], fantasy, feelings [fear])

The Fortune-Tellers by Lloyd Alexander, illustrated by Trina Schart Hyman: A carpenter who is unhappy with his trade goes to a fortune-teller to find out what the future holds for him. The fortune-teller predicts that he will be rich and happy. After he is mistaken for the fortune-teller by the landlady, he settles into this new trade, telling all his new customers the same fortune that he himself was told. He fulfills the prophecy and ends up rich and happy. (theme: fairy tale)

STORYPICKS

Come for a Ride on the Ghost Train by Colin and Jacqui Hawkins

Make Way for Ducklings by Robert McCloskey

ACTIVITIES

Game
After doing the crafts activity below, sing a variation of "Old MacDonald Had a Farm" where each person gets to hold up the animal he or she has created (see below) and lead the group for one verse of the song.

Crafts
Create farm animals together. You can use cotton balls, tissue paper, etc.. Cut-up pieces of paper to glue onto the animals and create the texture of fur or feathers.

Outside
Go outside, sit in a circle, and listen to the sounds of your neighborhood. Encourage each person to select one sound, and ask the person next to him or her to begin a story about what caused the sound. Continue the story as you go around the circle, ending with the person who started. Take turns so that there is a story for each person's sound.

SHOW NUMBER 128

Summary

James and Kino disagree on their favorite pizza topping. They decide to read a book, since reading is something they do agree on. James reads a book about a noisy little girl and another about seven brothers who help each other out. Then Carl comes in to read a book about a very loud ant.

Guest Readers

Carl Weintraub

 ## BOOKS READ

Noisy Nora by Rosemary Wells: Nora always has to wait while her parents are busy with her other siblings, either taking care of the baby or reading to the oldest. So Nora makes noises to make people notice her. When her family tells her to be quiet, she decides to disappear. But the family misses her so much that she decides to come back. (themes: family, feelings [being left out], rhyme)

The Seven Chinese Brothers by Margaret Mahy, illustrated by Jean and Mou-sien Tseng: Seven brothers in China have special supernatural powers that allow them to help each other in times of danger and need. One by one they help defend each other against the evil Emperor until they are all reunited at the Great Wall. (themes: family [siblings], resourcefulness, cooperation)

Effie by Beverley Allinson, illustrated by Barbara Reid: Effie the ant has a very loud voice. She makes so much noise that the other ants and insects run from her. She searches and searches to find someone who will listen to her, but she is just too loud. Then the shadow of a big foot falls across the ants. Effie uses her loud voice to tell the foot to stop, and all the ants are saved from being crushed. (themes: nature, problem-solving, differences)

 ## STORYPICKS

Lon Po Po translated and illustrated by Ed Young

The Tub People by Pam Conrad, illustrations by Richard Egielski

ACTIVITIES

Game
Have participants invent seven Chinese brothers and sisters, like the ones in the book. They should think up a special power for each. They should think of different powers than those in the book. Then they could each, in turn, act out the power of one of the siblings.

Crafts
Give each child a small round piece of cardboard with a small hole punched into it at one end. Have the children draw themselves doing something special that they know how to do. Use yarn to turn it into a necklace that will serve as a reminder of some of the special things that each child knows how to do.

Outside
Use the story Effie as a guide for an outdoor game. Kids can take turns playing Effie, and an adult can serve as the big foot. Let children experiment with very loud (outside) voices and very soft (inside) voices.

SHOW NUMBER 129

Summary

Kino is having a hard time putting together an alphabet book he made for Lucy's birthday. Mara helps him out and reads her own present to Lucy, which is an Amish alphabet book. Just as they finish wrapping their presents, Lucy comes back with her friend Diane, who reads from a book she wrote based on a story from Haiti. Then there is a picture book visit with Rae'Ven, who reads a book about lost teeth.

Guest Readers

Lucy

Rae'Ven Kelly

 **BOOKS READ**

The Folks in the Valley by Jim Aylesworth, illustrated by Stefano Vitale: This colorful alphabet book is filled with objects and activities from Amish life. (themes: alphabet, differences)

The Banza by Diane Wolkstein, illustrated by Marc Brown: A tiger and a goat are friends on the island of Haiti. The tiger gives the goat a banjo to protect her. He tells her to play the banjo over her heart, and one day they will be one. The goat learns to sing beautiful songs with the banjo. One day, the goat is surrounded by a group of ferocious tigers. She places the banjo over her heart and sings. This gives her the strength to scare the tigers away. (themes: friendship, feelings [courage], fairy tale)

Rosie's Baby Tooth by Maryann MacDonald, illustrated by Melissa Sweet: When Rosie's baby tooth comes out, she doesn't want to give it to the tooth fairy, so she tells her family that her tooth is lost. Her parents suggest she write to the tooth fairy. The tooth fairy writes back to offer a chain for her tooth, if she should happen to find it. In the morning, under Rosie's pillow, there is a new gold chain holding her baby tooth. (themes: family, identity [growing up])

 **STORYPICKS**

Animalia by Graeme Base

Dogger by Shirley Hughes

ACTIVITIES

Game
Have an "alphabet treasure hunt." Assign people different letters, and have them find objects in the room that begin with their letter. Then line all the objects up in alphabetical order while singing the ABC song.

Crafts
Create a list of ideas from all of the children as to how they can make a special alphabet book. Using this list of ideas, create a colorful alphabet book together. Keep the book on hand so that the children will always be able to look at it and remember that they helped to plan it as well as to make it.

Outside
Play the Tiger and Goat Banjo game. Some people can be tigers, who are slowly approaching the other people, who are goats. At various times, before an attack can occur, play a tape of banjo music (or you can clap your hands loudly), which will be the signal for the tigers to retreat.

Summary

Kino thinks he saw a yellow spaceship, but Mara doesn't believe him. Then they hear a noise. Michael comes to read them a story about visitors from a flying saucer and another one about some lazy animals who let their friend, the hen, do all the work. They all talk about how if you want to eat cake, you have to do the work. Tom comes in to read a book he wrote; then he puts the words to music.

Guest Readers

Mara

 **BOOKS READ**

Company's Coming by Arthur Yorinks, illustrated by David Small: One day a spaceship lands in Shirley and Moe's yard. When strange-looking visitors arrive, asking to use the bathroom, Moe is suspicious. He calls in the Army and the FBI, who quickly surround the house. Then Shirley opens the present the aliens brought and she finds that it is just what she needs — a new blender. Everyone can now relax and enjoy dinner with the visitors. (themes: sharing, differences)

The Little Red Hen by Paul Galdone: A cat, a dog, a mouse, and a hen all live together in a house, but the hen does all of the work. After the animals refuse to help the hen tend her wheat, which she bakes into a delicious cake, she announces that since she did all the work, she will eat the cake all by herself. From then on, all the animals are eager to help with household chores. (themes: cooperation, responsibility)

Engelbert the Elephant by Tom Paxton, illustrated by Steven Kellogg: Engelbert receives an invitation to the queen's ball. He practices and prepares a costume, but when the big day arrives, people run away from him in fear. The queen orders the horrified guests not to panic and invites Engelbert to dance. Engelbert is the hit of the party, and, after the ball, he and the guests join his friends from the jungle outside. (themes: adventure, rhyme, differences)

STORYPICKS

The Frog Prince Continued by Jon Scieszka, paintings by Steve Johnson

The True Story of the Three Little Pigs by A. Wolf as told to Jon Scieszka, illustrated by Lane Smith

ACTIVITIES

Game

Assign each person a food category (fruits, desserts, vegetables, etc.) and ask the children to think of as many foods as they can to fit their category. Afterward, you can plan pretend menus from the lists. Note: You can cut out a copy of the Food Pyramid from the side of most cereal boxes and use those food groups as your categories.

Crafts

Give each child an index card on which to draw a favorite food. On separate large pieces of poster board, write the names of each of the categories used in the game. When the children have finished with their drawings, ask them to tape their cards under the appropriate categories.

Outside

Act out *Company's Coming*. Some children can be the aliens, some can be the federal agents and the army, and two can play Shirley and Moe.

SHOW NUMBER 131

Summary

Kino is hungry. Lucy and Mara offer to share the gazpacho they are eating, but Kino doesn't want to try cold soup. Then there is a picture book visit to a farm where Sunni reads a story about pigs. Afterward, Kino is still hungry, so Mara offers him some of her fruit salad. The other kids try a taste too. Mara and Kino sing "The Itsy Bitsy Spider," then Paul comes to read a story. He is eager to try some gazpacho and encourages Kino to try new things too. Kino still isn't ready for gazpacho, so Paul reads his story about a magic bottle. Lucy returns with the gazpacho, and everybody has a taste, even Kino.

Guest Readers

Sunni Walton

Paul Winfield

📖 BOOKS READ

The Itsy Bitsy Spider by Iza Trapani: This illustrated version of the popular song with hand motions adds a few extra verses. After a series of unsuccessful climbs, the spider finally makes it to the top of the maple tree, spins a web, and takes a nice rest in the sun. (themes: nature, music)**

All Pigs Are Beautiful by Dick King-Smith, illustrated by Anita Jeram: A little girl who loves pigs talks about all the pigs she likes, what they do, and who they look like. Although she loves all pigs, her favorites are a black-and-white medium-snouted breed from Gloucester, and Monte, a gentle bull who loves to be scratched on top of his head and lives in the woods. (themes: animals, nature)

Do Not Open by Brinton Turkle: Miss Moody lives by the sea with her cat, Captain Kidd. She loves the sea and especially the wild storms that bring in wonderful things like a banjo clock that she cannot get to work. One day she finds a purple bottle with the words "Do Not Open." A voice from the bottle offers Miss Moody anything she wants if she opens the stopper. A mean-looking cloud of smoke with a monster face and a terrible voice emerges to frighten Miss Moody. She tricks him into turning into a mouse, who is promptly eaten by Captain Kidd. When they return home, Miss Moody finds that her treasured banjo clock is working for the first time. (themes: fantasy, curiosity, feelings [courage])

📖 STORYPICKS

Charlie Parker Played Be Bop by Chris Raschka

Pig Pig Grows Up by David McPhail

ACTIVITIES

Game
Play the spiderweb game with a ball of yarn. Gather the group in a circle. The ball of yarn will be thrown back and forth across the circle until a big "spider's web" is made in the center. Start by giving the end of the yarn to one person. While holding onto the end, the person should throw the ball of yarn to whomever the leader identifies. For example, the leader could say "Throw the ball to the person with blue shoes," or "...brown hair," or "...who has a new baby brother." Each time, whoever catches the yarn should hold on to a piece and throw the ball to the next person. You can continue this game until every person has had one, two, or three turns, and a large web has been created.

Crafts
Show children how to make "wacky" clocks out of circular pieces of paper. They could make face clocks, banjo clocks, or anything they can think of. Optional: Draw hands on the clocks, and use this opportunity to discuss how a clock works.

Outside
Take a walk after it has rained. Have the children look for things that have been caused by the rain, such as puddles, or changes that have occurred since it rained.

SHOW NUMBER 132

Summary

Kino has poison oak, and he can't stop itching. To comfort him, Mara reads him a special book based on a Spanish poem. Kino recites his own poem, then Liz comes in, greeting them in Spanish. She reads a book about a little boy who wants to be an artist. Kino thinks it's so good he forgets to scratch. Mara teaches him a clapping game to distract him, then they take a picture book visit with Wilford, who reads a book about a gorilla.

Guest Readers

Liz Torres

Wilford Brimley

B-64

📖 BOOKS READ

The Woman Who Outshone the Sun based on a poem by Alejandro Cruz Martinez, pictures by Fernando Olivera: One day a beautiful unknown woman comes to a small town in the country. She is so beautiful that she is said to outshine the sun. But because she is different, some people in the town drive her away. She washes her hair in the river for the last time, but the river stays in her hair and she must take it with her when she goes. When the people realize they have lost their river, they set out to bring her back. She forgives them, the river is returned, and the people learn to accept her. (themes: fairy tale, differences)

The Art Lesson by Tomie dePaola: All of Tomie's friends can do special things, but what he wants to do is to be an artist. From his cousins in art school he learns to practice, practice, practice, and never to copy. He can't wait for first grade when he will have his first art lesson with a real art teacher. However, when she comes, her assignment is to copy, and she won't let him use his sixty-four crayons. Finally, she agrees to let him draw whatever he wants if he completes the assignment first. (themes: uniqueness, determination)

Gorilla by Anthony Browne: Hannah loves gorillas, but she never gets to see them because her father is always working. She hopes to get a real gorilla for her birthday, but, when the day arrives, all she finds is a small toy gorilla at the foot of her bed. During the night, the toy grows and grows to become a real gorilla. Hannah and the gorilla take a trip to the zoo, to the movies, to a restaurant, and to dance on the lawn. In the morning, the gorilla becomes a toy again, but father agrees to take Hannah to the zoo. (themes: family [father], feelings [loneliness], fantasy)

📖 STORYPICKS

Harold and the Purple Crayon story and pictures by Crockett Johnson

Arrow to the Sun by Gerald McDermott

ACTIVITIES

Game
After the crafts activity below, use the fish (see below) to play a game about *The Woman Who Outshone the Sun*. Draw a small woman with a huge head of hair. Let the players take turns rolling dice. If they roll an odd number, they add that many fish to the hair; if it is an even number, they take away that many. (You may have to tell children whether the number is odd or even.)

Crafts
Encourage the children to create all kinds of small, colorful fish. They can be painted, crayoned, or glued with sparkles.

Outside
Take a field trip to the zoo. As a special focus, try observing animal communication, such as those of parent and child, friends, siblings, and different animals who live together.

Guest Readers

Mara

Summary

Kino and Mara have each invited some friends to Storytime. Mara's friend, Felton, talks about some of his favorite books when he was a child and then reads a book about a dog who rides around in a taxi. He reads another about a boy who doesn't want to clean his room. Kino's friend Katherine reads a book about a little cat who says no and another about a little girl who has a whale in her pond.

📚 BOOKS READ

The Adventures of Taxi Dog by Debra and Sal Barracca, pictures by Mark Buehner: Maxi is a stray dog wandering around New York City until he is picked up by Jim, a taxi driver. Together they travel the streets of New York picking up new people and taking them to new places across town. Maxi is happy to have finally found someone to take care of him. (themes: friendship, adventure, rhyme)

Clean Your Room, Harvey Moon by Pat Cummings: It is Saturday morning, and Harvey Moon wants to watch his favorite cartoons, but first he has to clean his room. Harvey races through the cleaning, pushing the mess under the rug so that he can watch TV. After examining his clean-up effort, his mother suggests that after lunch they start cleaning the lumps under his rug. (themes: responsibility, rhyme)

The Baby Blue Cat Who Said No by Ainslie Pryor: Mama takes very good care of her four baby cats. All of her babies love her dinner and her bedtime story except Baby Blue Cat, who says no. After the others are in bed, the Baby Blue Cat sees how sad he has made his mother, and he is very sorry. Together they finish the dinner and the story. Afterward the Mama cat asks him if he is sleepy, and once again he says no. (themes: family [mother], uniqueness, interactive story)

Dear Mr. Blueberry by Simon James: A little girl who loves whales carries on a correspondence with Mr. Blueberry about the whale she seems to have in her pond. With each of her letters, he writes back that what she has described is impossible, and each time she responds with a new observation about her whale. Then one day her whale moves on to another body of water, and she is very sad. When she sees her whale again at the beach, she sends love from herself and Mr. Blueberry. (themes: fantasy, nature)

STORYPICKS

Clifford the Big Red Dog by Norman Bridwell

Millions of Cats by Wanda Gág

ACTIVITIES

Game

After reading *Clean Your Room, Harvey Moon*, make a game out of cleaning up. Tell the group that they have five minutes to clean up. After each minute, ring a bell. When they hear the bell, they should freeze until you ring it again, signaling that they can clean again.

Crafts

Ask children to write (or dictate) or draw on a postcard (see below) to be sent to a family member or friend who lives out of town. They should obtain addresses in advance. When they have finished their postcards, let them put stamps on them and mail them.

Outside

Take a trip to a store to buy a postcard for each child to use in the crafts activity. After buying the postcards, you could visit the post office to purchase stamps. (Call in advance to see if you can take a tour of the post office.)

B-67

SHOW NUMBER 134

Summary

Kino arrives a little late, but just in time to hear the first story about a streetwise New York City dog. The kids talk about their favorite animals and move on to read a story about a cool mouse. Kino puts on his sunglasses to get in the mood. For the last book, about kids who share a batch of cookies, a teacher from Kino's school distributes cookies to everyone.

Guest Readers

Gedde Watanabe

 ## BOOKS READ

Maxi, the Hero by Debra and Sal Barracca, illustrated by Mark Buehner: This story, told in rhyme, follows the adventures of Maxi, who rides around New York City in a taxi with his friend Jim, the driver. When they come upon a woman whose purse has been stolen, Maxi chases the thief until the police arrive to take him away. Maxi is a hero. (themes: rhyme, concern for others)

Broderick by Edward Ormondroyd, illustrated by John Larrecq: Broderick is a mouse who loves to eat books, until one day he comes upon a story about mice. He reads about the adventures of other mice, and, despite the laughter of his peers, he decides to go out and do something different. He practices to become a surfer and soon becomes good enough to travel across the world with his partner and manager, Tim. He returns home a wealthy and successful hero. (themes: determination, identity)

The Doorbell Rang by Pat Hutchins: A mother has baked a big batch of cookies for her children at teatime. But the doorbell keeps ringing, each time bringing more children and causing them to divide the cookies to share. Finally Grandma comes, with enough of her cookies for everyone. (themes: friendship, sharing, counting, interactive story)**

STORYPICKS

Anatole by Eve Titus, pictures by Paul Galdone

Frederick by Leo Lionni

ACTIVITIES

Game
On a roll of paper, have everyone draw scenes that would be seen from the window of a taxi. Be sure to leave a few inches between each picture. Place a large drawing of a taxi (with cutouts for windows) over the drawings and move it or roll the paper so that the scenes are exposed as if the vehicle were driving.

Crafts
Bake pretend cookies. Cut out round shapes from brown paper bags, and have the children draw chocolate chips, raisins, or other favorite toppings on their "cookies."

Outside
Go outside, read the story of *Broderick*, and then act it out by pretending to make a surfboard, travel on a bus to the ocean, and surf.

SHOW NUMBER 135

Storytime

Guest Readers

Fred Savage

Steve Guttenberg

Summary

Kino has brought a really heavy book to the Storyplace, and Mara helps him take it out of his backpack. It is a book of poems and songs about America that was given to Kino by his grandfather, who read it as a young boy. Mara knows one of the songs, so she and Kino sing "The Erie Canal." Kino wants to sing it again, but Fred is ready to read a book about a boy who loses his mitten. They talk about how this story couldn't have happened, because it was just fantasy. Then Leah comes in to read two of the books she has written in rhyme. She asks the kids what it means to be cool and provides them all with sunglasses to read her first book, about a cool boy who does fantastic things. Her second book is about a best friend who has to move away. Finally, they all go on a picture book visit with Steve, who reads a book about snake brothers who learn to share.

B-70

BOOKS READ

The Mitten by Jan Brett: A little boy asks his grandmother to make him a snow-white mitten. She warns him that he will lose it if he takes it outside in the snow. When he loses the mitten, a growing crowd of animals crawls into it—a mole, a snow rabbit, a hedgehog, an owl, a badger, a fox, and a bear. Then a mouse crawls in and tickles the bear's nose, causing him to sneeze. The mitten is blown loose, the boy reclaims it, and the grandmother wonders why it is so much bigger than the other. (themes: responsibility, animals, sequence of events)

Earl's Too Cool for Me by Leah Komaiko, illustrated by Laura Cornell: Told in rhyme, with the title phrase as a chorus, this story is about a boy named Earl, a cool kid who has done a series of amazing things. An admiring friend finds that, as cool as Earl is, he is also nice and that the two of them can become friends. (themes: rhyme, friendship, interactive story)

Annie Bananie by Leah Komaiko, illustrated by Laura Cornell: Also in rhyme, this story is about two friends who have done many adventurous things together. Then Annie Bananie has to move away, and her friend assures her that while she may find some new friends in her new home, Annie will never, ever find a friend as good as her. (themes: friendship, rhyme)

Slither McCreep and His Brother Joe by Tony Johnston, illustrated by Victoria Chess: Slither McCreep and His Brother Joe are snakes whose major form of communication is squeezing. When Joe refuses to share his toys one day, their mother tells Slither to ignore him. But Slither retaliates by squeezing each toy until it breaks. His mother sends him to his room, where after some time to reflect, he breaks his piggy bank in order to replace the broken toys. (themes: family [siblings], sharing, responsibility)

STORYPICKS

A Day with Wilbur Robinson by William Joyce

Leo, the Late Bloomer by Robert Kraus, illustrated by Jose Aruego

ACTIVITIES

Game

In this game, you will act like Slither McCreep and squeeze things. Put everyday objects into balloons, and knot the balloon end closed. Ask the players to feel each one and try to figure out what is inside. You can use flour, rice, buttons, crayons, etc.

Crafts

Make a mitten bag by cutting out two mitten shapes from a piece of felt or cloth. Sew the pieces together and turn them inside out. Attach a string from both sides of the wrist to make a bag that can be filled with toy animals, vehicles, personal objects, etc. (This could be adapted to a younger age group by using glue instead of needle and thread.)

Outside

When the children are outside, preferably on a snowy or other wintery day, they can play the mitten game. After a child has dropped a mitten, the other kids can become animals. Make sure that the mitten is returned to its rightful owner.

Summary

Guest Readers

Kim Karnsrithong

Paula Poundstone

Kim and her cousin have stopped by for a visit. Kino explains that he has ten dollars saved up from doing some jobs for his mother, but he doesn't know what to spend it on. After Kim points out that he only has nine dollars, Lucy suggests that he save his money for a rainy day. While Kino decides what to do, Kim reads a book about a little girl with a pesky little brother. Paula comes in to read and suggests that Kino use his money to buy books. Paula reads a book about a restaurant for animals, and Kino points out that Storytime is just like the restaurant, where everyone is welcome. Finally Paula reads a book about a little girl who doesn't like her name, and everyone talks about nicknames.

 **BOOKS READ**

My Little Brother by Debi Gliori: A little girl is irritated by her pesky little brother and tries a variety of magic spells to try to get rid of him. Nothing works. Then one night she wakes up to find that his bed is empty. Suddenly she remembers how nice he was and how much she loves him. When she finds him asleep with the cat in the linen closet, she is so relieved that she realizes she doesn't want him to disappear after all. (themes: family [siblings], feelings [love])

Dinner at the Panda Palace by Stephanie Calmenson, illustrated by Nadine B. Westcott: A special restaurant run by Mr. Panda welcomes any and all animals. A variety of animals arrive for dinner in different numbers. When all fifty-five animal diners have sat down to eat, there is a knock at the door, and one little mouse asks if there is room for one more. Mr. Panda finds him his very own seat. (themes: rhyme, counting, animals)**

Chrysanthemum by Kevin Henkes: A little mouse is named Chrysanthemum by her parents—a perfect name for their perfect baby. As she grows, Chrysanthemum thinks her name is perfect too, until the day she goes to school and she is teased. Now she hates her name and doesn't think it's so perfect anymore. When Mrs. Twinkle, the pregnant new music teacher whom everyone admires, learns of Chrysanthemum's problem, she announces that she herself has a long name, Delphinium. If her baby is a girl, she will name her Chrysanthemum. Now Chrysanthemum loves her name and thinks it is just perfect again. (themes: feelings [teasing, embarrassment], self-esteem)

STORYPICKS

Train Leaves the Station by Eve Merriam, illustrated by Dale Gottlieb

Now Everybody Really Hates Me by Jane Read Martin and Patricia Marx, illustrated by Roz Chast

ACTIVITIES

Game
In a circle, have each member of the group identify something that he or she doesn't like. After all the children identify something, ask them to think of a part of that thing that they do like or that is good for them. For example, a sibling who bothers them may also be fun to play with, or a vegetable they don't like might be good for them.

Crafts
Ask the children to make name tags using stickers or paper. Make it into a necklace with yarn. They can wear their name tags for the day or take them home to put on their doors. (They can also ask their parents about the origin of their names.)

Outside
On a nice day, have a snack outside. As in *Dinner at the Panda Palace*, encourage the children to make entrances one at a time as animals with stories about what they were doing before coming to eat.

SHOW NUMBER 137

Summary

Guest Readers

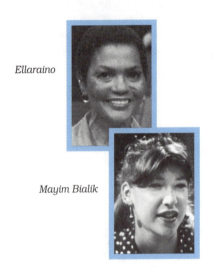

Ellaraino

Mayim Bialik

Ellaraino and Jenna arrive at the empty Storyplace and make themselves comfortable by reading a book about a little boy waiting for his father to come home. Mara returns with Kino, who missed the first story because he overslept. Mayim reads everybody a book about a cat who looks for his purr and another about Goldilocks and the Three Bears.

 ## BOOKS READ

First Pink Light by Eloise Greenfield, illustrated by Jan Spivey Gilchrist: A young boy is eager to stay up all night and wait for his father, who has been away for a month taking care of his grandmother. His mother wants the boy to go to bed, but he insists on surprising his father with his new hideout made of cardboard boxes. The mother allows him to wait in the rocking chair with a pillow, but he falls asleep and doesn't hear his father come home at dawn to carry him to his bed. (themes: family [father], feelings [excitement])

The Cat Who Lost His Purr by Michelle Coxon: One morning a cat named Boodle wakes up without his purr. He sets out to look for his purr in the quiet and empty house. It's not the drip in the bathroom faucet, the hum of the refrigerator, the tick of the cuckoo clock, or the fly buzzing past. When his unfurry friends come home, he is so happy to see them, he finds that his purr has returned with them. (themes: sounds, family, animals)

Goldilocks and the Three Bears retold and illustrated by Jan Brett: In a house in the woods lives a small bear, a medium-sized bear, and a big bear. Each one has a bowl, a chair, and a bed. One morning, after pouring hot porridge into their bowls, the bears go for a walk in the forest while the porridge cools. Goldilocks wanders in and eats the small bowl of porridge, breaks the small chair, and falls asleep in the small bed. When the bears come home they are confused, until they find the little girl fast asleep. When she is wakened, Goldilocks is frightened and runs away into the forest. (themes: fairy tale, responsibility, size)

 ## STORYPICKS

Cloudy with a Chance of Meatballs by Judi Barrett, drawn by Ron Barrett

The Biggest Bear by Lynd Ward

ACTIVITIES

Game

Paste animal pictures on index cards and place them in a box. In a circle, pass the box around, and have each person reach in and take one index card. Ask the child to then make the special sound of that animal, while the others guess which animal it is. Keep passing the box around until each person has had a turn.

Crafts

Make cat pictures on thick paper. After the drawing or painting is finished, staple two or three pipe cleaners onto the "cat's" nose. These whiskers will make the picture into a three-dimensional and adjustable piece of art. (You can purchase pipe cleaners inexpensively from a crafts supply store or from a store that sells pipes or tobacco.)

Outside

Ask the children to find small, medium, and large versions of several items outside (a twig, stone, leaf, etc.). They can simply lay them out or work together to find and place them in a bear house like the one in Goldilocks. The "house" can be located in the nooks and crannies made by playground equipment, such as under a slide or park bench.

Summary

Kino explains that he was late for Storytime because he had to help out at the zoo. Mara has a hard time believing his story. They talk about fiction and imagination, and Kino reads a story about a big lie. Kino asks for another story, so Vicki comes in with a group of kids to read a book about a little girl who is perfect. Kino announces that he is special, even if he's not perfect. He knows because his mother told him so. Then Alaina reads a book about a boy and his grandmother in South Africa.

Guest Readers

Vicki Juditz

Alaina Reed Hall

 ## BOOKS READ

A Big Fat Enormous Lie by Marjorie Weinman Sharmat, illustrated by David McPhail: A little boy is very sorry that he told a lie — he said he didn't eat all the cookies, but he did. Now the lie is getting bigger and uglier, and it won't go away. Finally, the boy gives up and tells his parents the truth. The lie starts to get smaller and smaller until it finally disappears. (themes: family, imagination, responsibility)

Super Dooper Jezebel by Tony Ross: Jezebel is perfect in every way at home and at school. Everyone calls her "Super Dooper Jezebel." She is so perfect that she gets a medal from the President, a statue is erected in her honor, and she goes on television to talk about herself. Then one day, the children are running and tell her to come too. Instructing them to walk, not run, she is snapped up by the crocodile they are fleeing, who has escaped from the zoo. (theme: uniqueness)

Not So Fast, Songololo by Niki Daly: Malousi lives in a big noisy family. They don't have much money, so he wears hand-me-down sneakers with big holes. One day his grandmother, GoGo, asks him to help her do some shopping in town. Along the way, they see a beautiful pair of red sneakers in the window. GoGo completes her errands in the big store and on the way back to the bus she buys the shoes for Malousi. He proudly marches home, and she struggles to keep up. (themes: family [grandmother], caring/concern for others)

STORYPICKS

Alexander and the Terrible, Horrible, No Good, Very Bad Day by Judith Viorst, illustrated by Ray Cruz

Mufaro's Beautiful Daughters by John Steptoe

ACTIVITIES

Game
Play the "nobody's perfect" game. Encourage every person to state one way in which he or she is not perfect. Then have someone tell one way in which that person is a great person.

Crafts
Ask each child to draw a picture of a boy or girl with or without cookies in his or her stomach. Cut out a piece of paper big enough to cover the stomach and tape over the first drawing. After the kids have drawn a shirt onto the flap, they can guess whether there are or are not cookies in the stomach.

Outside
Play a variation on "red-light/green-light". As in *Super Dooper Jezebel*, make believe a crocodile is chasing the children, but the children can only run when you give them the green light.

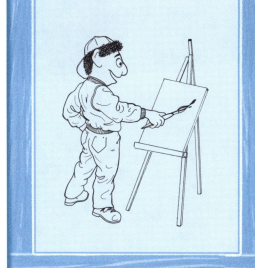

SHOW NUMBER 139

Summary

Kino reads a silly poem about a dog who flies to the moon. Then Ping Wu enters the Storyplace doing the dance of the moving mountain and reads a story from China. Glynn comes with Delina to read a book about a boy and a ghost. They all talk about ghosts, and Mara says she isn't afraid because ghosts are not real. Finally there is a picture book visit with Lucy, who reads a book about making life fun.

Guest Readers

Ping Wu

Glynn Turman

B-78

BOOKS READ

Ming Lo Moves the Mountain by Arnold Lobel: Ming Lo and his wife live at the bottom of a large mountain, where large rocks constantly fall on his house and the shadows cover his garden. Ming Lo goes to the wise man to ask how to move the mountain. After trying different things, Ming Lo follows the wise man's suggestion to take apart his house, tie all the pieces together, then walk backward with his eyes closed. When he walks far enough, he can open his eyes and rebuild his house in a spot that is no longer in the shadow of the big mountain. (themes: fairy tale, problem-solving)

The Boy and the Ghost by Robert D. San Souci, illustrated by J. Brian Pinkney: Thomas is from a poor family with seven children who live in a tumbledown house. He resolves to go to the big city to make money for his family and meets a man who tells him about the haunted house of a rich man who has died. It is said that the one who can stay in the house from sunset to sunrise will get all of the riches in the house. Settling into the house, Thomas makes some soup, which he offers to a ghost, who in return shows Thomas where to find a pot of gold. Thomas gives half of the gold to the poor and keeps the rest for his family, who lives happily in the large house. (themes: family, fantasy, responsibility, feelings [courage])

Life Is Fun by Nancy Carlson: This book is a list of instructions for living on earth and being happy. Be nice, eat healthy food once in a while, get exercise, feel free to cry when you are sad, laugh a lot, fall in love, and you will be awesome. (theme: feelings [happiness])

STORYPICKS

The Polar Express by Chris Van Allsburg

The Legend of Bluebonnet retold and illustrated by Tomie dePaola

ACTIVITIES

Game
Create a list of things that can go wrong in a house or apartment, one item from each participant. After the list is finished, work together to think up solutions to each of the problems. When a solution has been found for each problem, the game is over.

Crafts
Each child should decorate one or more links that will go into a chain made of construction paper. Each link should represent something in the child's home. Put the links together, and see how far the chain can go.

Outside
Following the ideas in *Life Is Fun*, go outside and get some exercise. One fun way is for the children to work together to create an obstacle course.

SHOW NUMBER 140

Summary

Rosalind comes to Storytime to read a story about a princess, a tale with a twist. After talking about how not everybody wants the same things in life, Jim reads a book about animals and their sounds. Kino tells a riddle, and they read another book, one about a friendship between a girl and her neighbor.

Guest Readers

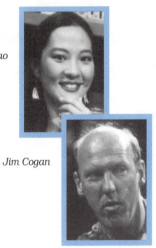

Rosalind Chao

Jim Cogan

 **BOOKS READ**

Princess Smartypants by Babette Cole: All the princes want to marry Princess Smartypants, but she has decided she never wants to get married. She likes being a Ms., and she wants to be independent. To keep them away, she creates impossible tasks that each one must accomplish in order to marry her. Then Prince Swashbuckle arrives and accomplishes all that she asks. But when she kisses him, he turns into a toad. Now no one wants to marry her anymore and she lives happily ever after by herself. (themes: fairy tale, uniqueness)

"Stand Back," Said the Elephant, "I'm Going to Sneeze!" by Patricia Thomas, pictures by Wallace Tripp: An elephant is about to sneeze, but all the animals beg him not to. Last time he sneezed, everything blew away, and it was a disaster. Then a mouse scares the elephant so much that he forgets to sneeze. The animals are saved until the elephant starts to laugh so hard that the earth begins to shake. (themes: rhyme, animals, cause and effect)

A Special Trade by Sally Wittman, pictures by Karen Gundersheimer: Bartholomew is Nellie's older neighbor. Throughout her life, he helped take care of her, taking her for walks in the carriage and cheering her up when she fell. Then Bartholomew, who is getting older, falls down the stairs and returns from the hospital in a wheelchair. Now it is Nellie's turn to take him for walks, just like he did for her. (themes: friendship, caring/concern for others)

STORYPICKS

Wilfred Gordon McDonald Partridge by Mem Fox, illustrated by Julie Vivas

The Paper Bag Princess story by Robert N. Munsch, art by Michael Martchenko

ACTIVITIES

Game
Play the "Mission Impossible" game. Like Princess Smartypants, ask the children to think up impossible tasks (challenging but safe). Make a list of the tasks. After each person has created one idea, everyone can discuss ways in which the tasks could actually be accomplished.

Crafts
Cut crowns out of paper and ask the children to decorate them with glitter, crayons, stickers, etc. They can then wear their crowns and pretend to be Princess Smartypants or one of the princes.

Outside
When playing outside, have the children take turns caring for each other as if they were injured. Let the kids be creative and have fun with it, and they will soon see that it takes hard work to help somebody who is in need.

Summary

Guest Readers

Tim Allen

Mara reminds everyone about the story of the three little pigs. They talk about who the good guy is and who the bad guy is in the story, because the version Mara tells is one with a twist. Then Tim arrives to read the same story, told from the side of the wolf. Now it's not so easy to see who the bad guy is.

 **BOOKS READ**

The Three Little Wolves and the Big Bad Pig by Eugene Trivizas illustrated by Helen Oxenbury: In this variation on *The Three Little Pigs*, three cuddly wolves out in the world on their own are warned to watch out for the big bad pig. After the pig destroys several houses they build, they build a beautiful but fragile house out of flowers. The pig is so taken by the smell of the flowers that his heart softens and he becomes a big good pig. He sings and dances and plays tag with the wolves, who invite him to stay on and live with them. (themes: fairy tale, friendship, feelings [surprise])

The True Story of the Three Little Pigs by A. Wolf as told to Jon Scieszka, illustrated by Lane Smith: Telling his side of the story, the wolf makes up a wild tale about how a big sneeze started all his troubles with the three little pigs. (themes: fairy tale, differences [perspective])

 **STORYPICKS**

Yo, Hungry Wolf by David Vozar, illustrated by Betsy Lewin

The Three Little Javelinas by Susan Lowell, illustrated by Jim Harris

ACTIVITIES

Game
Place the names and pictures of various animals into a cloth bag. Have each person pick out one and think of a way in which that animal could help the three little pigs. For example, an eagle could fly them away or a horse could carry them away from the wolf.

Crafts
Make hand puppets out of socks. The children can use permanent markers to create the nose and the mouth. Yarn hair can be glued on top, and with older children, buttons can be used for the eyes. The puppets can be people, animals, or made-up characters.

Outside
Play a version of *The Three Little Pigs/Wolves*. Divide the group into two, with half as wolves and half as pigs. First the innocent pigs will be trapped by the bad wolves, and then the nice wolves will be surrounded by the mean pigs. Before the game all of the children can work together on building the house.

SHOW NUMBER
202

Summary

Kino models his spring pageant costume, which he doesn't like because of the flower headdress. Mara reads a story, and a bad day is turned into a good day. They fix the costume, and Kino agrees to do the best job he can. This reminds Mara of the next book, about a little boy trying to grow a flower, which is read by Robert. Kino returns from the pageant with Annie, and she reads a bedtime book to Kino and her son.

Guest Readers

Robert Guillaume

Annie Potts

B-84

BOOKS READ

Regina's Big Mistake by Marissa Moss: Today the class has an assignment to draw the jungle or the rain forest, but Regina just can't start to draw. When she finally does start, she makes a mistake. She tries to erase it but the paper rips, and she ruins the sun by making it look like a crescent. The teacher says she can't have any more paper, and the other kids laugh at her sun. Then she decides to make her funny sun a moon and make the picture a nighttime one. Now she thinks her drawing is perfect. (themes: self-esteem, uniqueness, problem-solving)

The Empty Pot by Demi: The emperor, who loves flowers, gives all the children one seed and says that the child with the best flower at the end of the year will succeed him. Ping, who also loves flowers, cannot make his seed grow and brings the empty pot to show the emperor. The emperor announces that he had handed out cooked seeds that could not grow. Only Ping was honest enough to tell the truth, and he is named the new emperor. (themes: responsibility, nature)

Wind Says Goodnight by Katy Rydell, illustrated by David Jorgensen: The wind outside tells the child to sleep in her bed. But the child cannot sleep because a number of insects and animals are all making noises. Finally, after the moon stops shining, all the animals stop their noises and the child can fall asleep. (themes: music, nature, sequence of events, problem-solving)

STORYPICKS

Goodnight Moon by Margaret Wise Brown, illustrated by Clement Hurd

K Is for Kiss Goodnight by Jill Sardegna, illustrated by Michael Hays

ACTIVITIES

Game
Play a version of *The Wind Says Goodnight*. One by one, in a circle, have each child say why he or she can't sleep. When you reach the last one, you can make everything stop so they can sleep. All can then pretend to fall asleep.

Crafts
Give the children pieces of paper that have "mistakes" on them. These mistakes can include splotches, random shapes, or small patches of scribble. The kids can then create a work of art that incorporates the mistake. After they have finished, point out to the children that what often seems like a mistake can be made useful.

Outside
Grow flowers or grass. Poke some holes into the bottom of clear plastic cups, and fill them three-quarters of the way with soil. Sprinkle with seeds, cover with a bit more soil, and water every day. By using plastic cups it is possible to see how the seeds grow below the surface as well as above.

SHOW NUMBER 203

Summary

Guest Readers

Little Richard

Mara and Kino are giving the library a spring cleaning. When Kino tries to fit too many books in his bag and it breaks, it makes him think about the story of the mitten. Mara thinks of another book, a story about a full little hut, so they decide to take a break to read it. Little Richard comes by to read the children a book about someone, like Kino, who didn't listen to advice. Then he reads and sings from another book, one about a grasshopper who doesn't listen and would rather play than work. This reminds Kino and Mara that it's time to get back to work.

 ## BOOKS READ

Knock, Knock, Teremok! adapted and illustrated by Katya Arnold: A series of progressively larger animals knock at the door of an empty hut and move in to stay. When a big bear arrives, the fly, who was the first one in, tells him there is no room. The bear tries to sit on the roof of the little hut, but the roof caves in. (themes: sharing, problem-solving, sequence of events)

Little Lumpty by Miko Imai: In the town of Dumpty, there is a big wall. All the children sing about Humpty Dumpty and his fall, but Little Lumpty dreams of someday climbing the wall too. One day, he brings a ladder and climbs to the top. Once on top, however, he is too scared to walk back to the ladder, and he can't come down. The whole town comes out to help and hold a blanket at the bottom for him to jump into. Little Lumpty is sorry he didn't listen, but he had to see the top of the wall. (themes: fairy tale, feelings [fear], adventure)

The Grasshopper and the Ants retold by Margaret Wise Brown, illustrated by Larry Moore: A grasshopper sings and dances all summer long while the ants are working hard storing up for the long winter. When winter comes and he is cold and has not worked to store up food, the grasshopper is allowed to live in the ants' warm house if he works in exchange for his shelter. The queen ant asks him to sing and play his music as their entertainment. From then on the grasshopper sings a different and more grateful tune. (themes: sharing, responsibility, music)

STORYPICKS

The Hobyahs by Robert D. San Souci, illustrated by Alexi Natchev

One Hundred Hungry Ants by Elinor J. Pinczes, illustrated by Bonnie MacKain

ACTIVITIES

Game

Play the *Little Lumpty* game. Use blocks to create a scale. Balance a long block on a small block at its center. One by one have the players place small objects that represent Lumpty onto the long block. The object of the game is for everyone to work together to keep it balanced and prevent Lumpty from falling off.

Crafts

Draw a simple hut on a huge piece of poster board. One at a time, let the children draw different animals inside the house until it resembles the hut in *Knock, Knock, Teremok!*

Outside

Take a walk outside, and look for ants. Take time to observe the ants closely, and let the children guess what they are doing.

SHOW NUMBER 204

Summary

Kino is miserable and lonely because he is sick in bed and cannot go to the Storyplace to hear stories. Then Lucy arrives to read him a book about a boy in the hospital. Kino cheers up a little when Jamie comes to read a book about learning to laugh. After a few days of rest, Kino is well enough to visit the zoo, where he reads a book about a strange animal.

Guest Readers

Jamie Walters

 ## BOOKS READ

Going Home by Margaret Wild, illustrated by Wayne Harris: Hugo is in the hospital and is eager to go home soon. His room looks over the zoo, and each night a new animal takes him for an adventure. The elephant takes him for a ride in the African plains, the howler monkey takes him to the Amazon jungle, and the snow leopard takes him to the Himalayas. When he tells his family about these visits, his sister is very jealous, because she only goes to the park or the store. On Hugo's last day at the hospital, he is getting ready to go to India. He tells the children in the nearby beds about his secret travels, and the next night they go with the tiger to India. (themes: imagination, feelings [homesickness], friendship, adventure)

The Tickleoctopus by Audrey Wood, illustrated by Don Wood: Millions of years ago, Bup the prehistoric boy lived with his ill-tempered parents. He is forced to do all the chores by himself, because his other siblings are gone. His parents, Ugma and Ugpa, lock him in a cave every day so that no one can take him. One day, one of his tears drops into the cave pond and a strange pink creature, the Tickleoctopus, emerges to tickle him. The Tickleoctopus causes everyone to laugh and smile, and one by one, the lost siblings return and everyone celebrates. (themes: family, feelings [happiness], fairy tale)

The Grumpalump by Sarah Hayes, illustrated by Barbara Firth: On the ground lies a big "grumpalump," or a lump that grumps. One by one, animals approach the grumpalump to determine what it is. No one could tell until the gnu blew and the lump started to expand and change shape. It starts to rise, and they see that it is a hot airship that flies off into the sky. (themes: rhyme, problem-solving)

STORYPICKS

Martha Calling by Susan Meddaugh

Is Your Mama a Llama? by Deborah Guarino, illustrated by Steven Kellogg

ACTIVITIES

Game
Pair people up and ask one person to make the other laugh or smile; then switch so the other person gets a turn. At the end, generate a list together of all the things that made the children smile or laugh.

Crafts
Help the children create original works of art to cheer up kids who are in the hospital. If they want to, they can write or dictate words of hope or encouragement as well. When they are all complete, send them all off to a local children's hospital or clinic.

Outside
Act out *The Grumpalump* story together. Playing as animals, the children will approach and inspect the mystery grumpalump. As an added bonus, you can accompany the drama with tape-recorded noises.

SHOW NUMBER 205

Summary

Guest Readers

Marion Ross

Lucy

Kino realizes that it is raining on Lucy's paintings, but she is so busy with her book she is not listening to him. Kevin helps Kino move the paintings out of the way so they don't get ruined. Marion reads them a book about people who work together, like Kevin and Kino did, to save a bird trapped on the subway. Lucy sends the boys for a visit with Don and Audrey in their studio, where they read a book they wrote and illustrated. When Kino and Kevin return to the Storyplace, there is a surprise. Lucy has made them Storytime superhero outfits to thank them for saving her paintings. Finally, they all read a book about a boy whose brother is older and smarter.

 ## BOOKS READ

Subway Sparrow by Leyla Torres: When a sparrow flies into a subway car, a little girl tries to help him escape. A man who only speaks Spanish tries to help her. When their attempts fail, a Polish woman suggests they use her scarf to hold the sparrow. Though each person speaks a different language, they are able to set the sparrow free outside the station. (themes: cooperation, problem-solving)

King Bidgood's in the Bathtub by Audrey Wood, illustrated by Don Wood: The page enlists the help of various members of the kingdom to help get the king out of the bathtub. Nothing that any of them can do convinces the king to get out until the page decides to pull the plug in the bathtub. (themes: interactive story, problem-solving, sequence of events)

Ollie Knows Everything by Abby Levine, illustrated by Lynn Munsinger: Herbert feels as though his older brother Ollie Knows Everything. Then, on a family trip to New York City, Ollie is left on the train, and the family is separated. Herbert feels sad as they search for Ollie. When the family returns to their hotel, they find Ollie waiting for them with a crowd of reporters and onlookers. Herbert realizes that Ollie does know everything, even how to get home by himself. (themes: family [siblings], feelings [fear, relief], problem-solving)

STORYPICKS

Supergrandpa by David M. Schwartz, illustrated by Bert Dodson

Three Cheers for Tacky by Helen Lester, illustrated by Lynn Munsinger

ACTIVITIES

Game
Divide the group into pairs. Give one member of each pair an instruction that he or she must convey to the other person without words. Sample tasks include setting up for a snack, building something specific with blocks, or cleaning up.

Crafts
Help the children create their own maps to imaginary places from the perspective of way up in the sky. Start by showing them sample road maps, subway maps, and library, store, or school maps. If they need help, suggest that they start by drawing a few sights as they think they would look if they were sitting in a cloud and then connecting them by roads. As a variation, they can make maps of their neighborhoods.

Outside
Play an "Ollie" version of hide-and-seek. The children will hide and seek as usual. When there are only two hidden children left, the seekers should share jokes and act silly within hearing distance of the last two children. Their laughter will help the seekers find them.

SHOW NUMBER 206

Summary

Guest Readers

Kirk Douglas

Kino and Lucy are playing in the snow, sledding, and building a snowman. Lucy is getting cold, so she lures Kino inside with a story about a hat in the snow. They read another about a boy who goes sledding. Afterward, Kino doesn't want to leave, but Lucy reminds him they have to meet Mr. Douglas at the Storyplace. Kino tries to bring back part of the snowman to show Mr. Douglas, but by the time they get there, all he has is a pail of water. After two more stories about the snow, Lucy suggests that Kino use the snowman water to water the plants.

 **BOOKS READ**

A Hat for Minerva Louise by Janet Morgan Stoeke: Minerva Louise is a hen who loves the snow. She wants to explore, but it is too cold. She needs to find a hat and tries different objects around the farmyard. Finally she finds just the right thing — a pair of mittens she can use, one to cover her head and the other her tail. (themes: adventure, problem-solving, resourcefulness)**

The Story of a Boy Named Will, Who Went Sledding Down the Hill by Daniil Kharms, translated by Jamey Gambrell, illustrated by Vladimir Radunsky: A boy named Will starts down the hill on his sled until he hits a hunter, who gets on the sled. They keep going until they hit a dog, who gets on, and they continue on until they hit a fox, a hare, and then a bear. After that ride, Will never rides his sled again. (themes: adventure, sequence of events)

Dogteam by Gary Paulsen, illustrated by Ruth Wright Paulsen: A team of dogs pulls a sled through a cold and snowy night, admiring and observing the winter forest landscape. (themes: feelings [happiness], nature, animals)

Prize in the Snow by Bill Easterling, illustrated by Mary Beth Owens: A young boy, eager to be a big hunter like the older kids, sets out one morning with a box and a carrot to catch a rabbit or a bird. When he manages to trap a rabbit, he slowly lifts the box so that the rabbit cannot escape. But when he looks inside, the rabbit stays still, looking skinny and cold. The boy offers the carrot to the rabbit and sets him free, promising to bring more food tomorrow. (themes: caring/concern for others, nature)

 **STORYPICKS**

The Five Dog Night by Eileen Christelow

Liplap's Wish by Jonathan London, illustrated by Sylvia Long

ACTIVITIES

Game
Divide a circle into four equal parts, each representing a different season. You can use masking tape on the floor to mark each quarter of the circle. Place a spinning object such as a plastic bottle in the center, and let each player have a chance to spin it. When it lands on a particular season, the person can say one thing he or she likes to do during that time of year. (If you want to make the game easier, use only winter and summer, and divide the circle in half.)

Crafts
Help the children create three-dimensional snow paintings. They can create outdoor scenes that take place in the snow. After the rest of the picture has been completed, they can glue cotton balls where the snow belongs. To create a "still snowing" effect, try gluing silver sprinkles or coarse salt on the painting.

Outside
Take a walk outside, and notice what kinds of animals and birds live in your neighborhood. Talk about which animals live in people's homes, such as dogs and cats, and which animals do not live in people's homes, such as squirrels and wild birds. When you get back, you could make a chart of the animals you saw.

SHOW NUMBER 207

Summary

Guest Readers

Teri Garr

Kirsten Dunst

Kino is dressed as The Amazing Kino, a magician. He tries to perform a magic trick for Teri and the kids, but it just isn't working. Teri suggests that he keep trying while she reads a book with magic in it, about time travel. Kino tries the trick again, but has no luck and goes to Mara for help. She has a book about an animal who tries hard to find some magic, just like Kino. Finally, there is a picture book visit with Kirsten, who reads a book about a little girl who learns that appearances aren't everything. Afterward, Kino tries his trick again, and this time it works.

 BOOKS READ

Time Train by Paul Fleischman, illustrated by Claire Ewart: A girl and her class take a train to learn more about dinosaurs. They head west to the Rocky Mountains, and by the time they get to Philadelphia, it seems to be the turn of the century. By the time they get to Pittsburgh, it is the Civil War. They spot a mammoth on the landscape. When they arrive at their destination they can't find a motel, so they sleep in a dinosaur's footprint, and for breakfast they have scrambled dinosaur eggs. They camp on the beach, and play ball with the dinosaurs, and one child goes flying by on the back of a pterodactyl. Finally, the train comes to take them back home. The kids have learned a lot more than they thought about dinosaurs on this trip. (themes: imagination, nature, adventure)

Pip's Magic by Ellen Stoll Walsh: Pip is a young lizard who is afraid of the dark. When his friends can't help him, he goes to the frogs, who suggest he ask old Abra the wizard for help. After a long trip through the woods, he finds Abra at sunrise and tells him of his fear of the dark. Abra tells him that Pip has the magic he needs for the dark — he found it in the dark woods, the tunnel, and the dark night of his journey. (themes: feelings [fear, courage], determination)

Cabbage Rose by M.C. Helldorfer, illustrated by Julie Downing: Cabbage is a plain-faced young girl visited by a magician who leaves her a new paintbrush that makes painted things become real. She goes to the marketplace where people are mesmerized by her painting and the prince asks her for twelve pictures. While she paints, he watches her in awe and tells her stories about love that make her blush. The prince calls her Cabbage Rose. Completing her pictures and realizing she will no longer see the prince, she paints herself as a beautiful lady and goes to the castle. But the prince asks her to paint Cabbage Rose. She breaks the brush, becomes herself again, and the old magic ends; but a new one begins as she is married to the prince and paints beside him and their children. (themes: family [siblings], uniqueness, fairy tale)

STORYPICKS

The Wizard by Bill Martin, Jr., illustrated by Alex Schaeffer

Can I Have a Stegosaurus, Mom? Can I? Please? by Lois G. Grambling, illustrated by H.B. Lewis

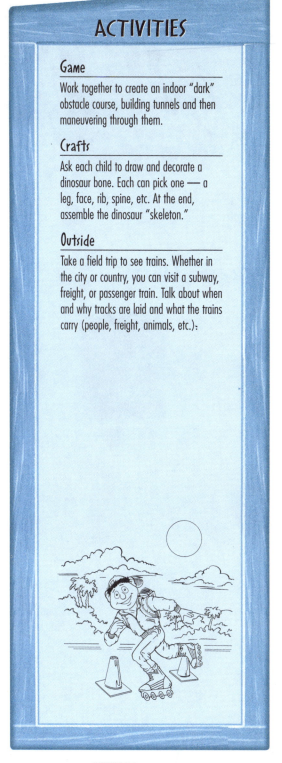

ACTIVITIES

Game
Work together to create an indoor "dark" obstacle course, building tunnels and then maneuvering through them.

Crafts
Ask each child to draw and decorate a dinosaur bone. Each can pick one — a leg, face, rib, spine, etc. At the end, assemble the dinosaur "skeleton."

Outside
Take a field trip to see trains. Whether in the city or country, you can visit a subway, freight, or passenger train. Talk about when and why tracks are laid and what the trains carry (people, freight, animals, etc.).

Guest Readers

Joanna Cassidy

Summary

Today, everyone at Storytime is dressed up like a character from his or her favorite book. Mara is dressed like a cat, and Kino is dressed up like a pickle for his favorite story about a pickle who takes everyone on a chase. He and the kids talk about this tall tale. Then Joanna comes in dressed like the swamp angel from a book about a giant woman who wrestles a bear.

 **BOOKS READ**

Stop That Pickle! by Peter Armour, illustrated by Andrew Shachat: Elmira Deeds goes to Mr. Adolf's deli to ask for a pickle. There is only one left in the jar, and Mr. Adolf just can't seem to spear it. This pickle does not want to be eaten, so he jumps out of the jar and runs out the door. He is chased by a variety of foods and finally collides with a boy and is knocked out. The boy is very hungry because he missed lunch, but the pickle cries, and the boy decides to eat all the other foods. After the ice cream, he realizes he can't eat a sour pickle, so the pickle is spared. (themes: adventure, sequence of events)

Swamp Angel by Anne Isaacs, illustrated by Paul O. Zelinsky: In 1815 in the Tennessee backwoods, Angel was born. She grew very fast and very large and saved the wagons of the pioneer settlers from being stuck in the mud. She became known as the Swamp Angel. Then the settlers were threatened by a huge bear named Tarnation. Many tried to catch the bear, but only Swamp Angel could do it. She won the bear's hide, which was so huge that she lay it out in front of her Montana cabin, where it became the western prairie. (themes: fairy tale, problem-solving, sharing)

STORYPICKS

Catkin by Antonia Barber, illustrated by P.J. Lynch

Harvey Potter's Balloon Farm by Jerdine Nolen, illustrated by Mark Buehner

John Henry by Julius Lester, illustrated by Jerry Pinkney

ACTIVITIES

Game
During snack time, create silly stories of how the food got there. Encourage people to use their imaginations and describe how the food got to the table, using *Stop That Pickle!* as an example. Each person should have at least one turn.

Crafts
Encourage each child to illustrate and cut out a different type of fruit, vegetable, or other food. Each item will have legs and be running. Assemble the items in a line on the wall so that they are all chasing after each other.

Outside
Take a field trip to a pond, lake, mountain, or other natural attraction in your area. When you get there, ask the children to imagine how it got its name.

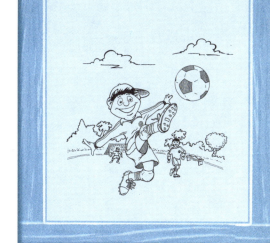

SHOW NUMBER 209

Summary

Guest Readers

Amy Hill

Kino is watching the fish in Lucy's tank as Lucy paints a seascape. He pretends he is a whale, having a race. Lucy reads Kino a story about whales, and they talk about imagination. Amy arrives with some kids and an imagination box with a surprise inside. She reads a story about a little girl who uses her imagination to make a special friend and another book about the sea and a little girl's favorite memories. Afterward, they open the imagination box, which contains materials to make anything they want.

 **BOOKS READ**

The Whales' Song by Dyan Sheldon, illustrated by Gary Blythe: Lily's grandmother tells her about the whales in the ocean outside the house. She explains that if you leave them a present, they will sing to you in return. Uncle Frederick thinks the story is silly and suggests that her grandmother tell Lily something useful about whales. Lily goes out to the dock to leave a yellow flower for the whales and waits all day for them to appear. That night she wakes up to hear them calling her name in the wind far away. (themes: family [grandmother], imagination, nature)

The Paper Princess by Elisa Kleven: A little girl makes a princess out of paper. Before she finishes the hair, the wind carries the paper princess away. She is found by a little girl who accidentally gives the princess green hair. A blue jay offers to help the princess find the little girl who made her, and they fly all over looking. They land in a meadow near a little boy. He brings the picture to his sister, who is the girl who made the princess. They are happily reunited. (themes: adventure, differences, friendship)

The Big Big Sea by Martin Waddell, illustrated by Jennifer Eachus: A little girl and her mother enjoy a special time together at the sea. They walk to the beach at night, walk in up to their ankles, splash in the water, and make footprints. Afterward her mother carries the little girl home for hot toast by the fire. (themes: family [mother], nature)**

STORYPICKS

Wanda's Roses by Pat Brisson, illustrated by Maryann Cocca-Leffler

Our Granny by Margaret Wild, illustrated by Julie Vivas

ACTIVITIES

Game
Play imaginary show-and-tell. Have each person pull an imaginary object out of a shoe box and tell everybody about what the object is or reminds them of.

Crafts
Help the children make paper princesses as in the story. Allow them to use any color of yarn, long or short, cotton balls, or any other materials to create texture or shape for the hair.

Outside
Visit a body of water. (Possible locations include a stream, river, lake, pond, or ocean.) Bring paper and crayons. Once there, discuss what makes that body of water special and ways in which it is different from other types of water. Encourage the children to make a drawing of what they see.

SHOW NUMBER 210

Summary

Guest Readers

Theresa Saldana

Kino has made himself a suit of shining armor out of tin plates and is pushing in a castle he has made out of a large box. He explains to Lucy that he has argued with his friend Jenny, who thought his castle looked like a fort. Now he is mad at her and wants to stay hidden in his castle. Lucy has a story about a brave little mouse to help bring him out. Kino is interested and even peeks out of the window. Then Theresa comes to read a book about two friends who are learning to take turns. Kino suggests that maybe next time he and Jenny can take turns calling the box a castle or a fort. Finally, Theresa reads another book, about the many different kinds of houses in the world.

BOOKS READ

Sheila Rae, the Brave by Kevin Henkes: Sheila Rae is not afraid of anything, not the dark, not the principal, not even the cracks in the sidewalk. One day, she decides to walk home a new way. She realizes that she does not know where she is and suddenly begins to hear scary noises. She stops to cry and call for her parents and her sister Louise. Louise, who has quietly followed behind, assures her that they are not lost and leads her sister home. (themes: family [siblings], feelings [fear, courage])

The Rat and the Tiger by Keiko Kasza: Rat and Tiger are best friends but somehow Rat always seems to get the short end of the stick. When they play, Rat always has to be the bad guy, and he always gets the smallest piece of food. But after he confronts Tiger, they get along, taking turns and splitting things down the middle. Now they have a new problem — there's a new rhino on the block. (themes: friendship, cooperation, size)

A House Is a House for Me by Mary Ann Hoberman, illustrated by Betty Fraser: This picture book describes in rhyme all the many kinds of houses for all the animals, vehicles, people, and things all over the earth. (themes: rhyme, vocabulary, nature)

STORYPICKS

Mr. Tall and Mr. Small by Barbara Brenner, illustrated by Mike Shenon

A Place for Grace by Jean Davies Okimoto, illustrated by Doug Keith

ACTIVITIES

Game
Divide the group into pairs. Randomly distribute mazes (see below) that the kids have created. Working in pairs, with a water-soluble marker, ask the kids to try to make it through the mazes.

Crafts
Show the children how to create simple mazes. They can use rulers for the straight lines and their imagination for the rest. Make sure that each maze has a beginning and an end, and that it is possible to travel all the way through it. Laminate the mazes so that, with the use of a water-soluble marker, they can be done over and over again. (You can have the mazes laminated at a copy shop, or check whether your local library can laminate for you.)

Outside
Build a house out of some of the materials that are normally used during outside play time. Encourage the group to think about what kind of house they will create, such as a farm house or animal home.

SHOW NUMBER
211

Summary

Guest Readers

Ruben Blades

Para Ti

Mara has brought Kino to visit a Spanish church so he can see what it is like. She tells him about her Christmases as a young girl, when she made tamales with her mother. They are joined by a little girl named Isabel who doesn't speak any English. They invite her to look at the pictures while they read a story in English about a little girl and the tamales she makes with her mother for Christmas. Mara invites Isabel to the Storyplace for more stories. Back at the Storyplace, Mara is teaching Kino "Jingle Bells" in Spanish. She promises that later they will have a party with tamales and a piñata. Isabel arrives as promised with Ruben, who has brought two books to read in Spanish. The first is a Spanish version of "The Little Red Hen," and the second is the Spanish version of a book about a little boy who has lost his teddy bear. After the stories, everyone is ready for the special party. Kino is the first to try to break the piñata.

B-102

📖 BOOKS READ

Too Many Tamales by Gary Soto, illustrated by Ed Martinez: Maria and her mother are making tamales for their big Christmas celebration with the relatives. She is proud to be a big girl and admires her mother's ring. While her mother goes to answer the phone, Maria tries the ring on. Then she realizes that the ring is lost, and thinking it has fallen into the tamales, she and her cousins eat all twenty-four tamales. But the ring is not found. She goes to tell her mother and notices the ring on her finger. It wasn't lost after all. All the grown-ups laugh as they head into the kitchen to make twenty-four more tamales. (themes: family, holidays [Christmas], problem-solving)

La Gallinita Roja by Margot Zemach: This is a Spanish-language version of the classic story about a little red hen who works hard to plant a seed of wheat, help it grow, harvest the crop, and bake a cake with the flour without the help of her lazy animal friends. (themes: cooperation, responsibility)

¿Donde Esta Mi Osito? by Jez Alborough: Eduardito has lost his teddy bear, Alfredito, and heads into the dark forest to find it. There he finds a large teddy bear, just like his own, which is too large to carry. Then he hears a loud noise, and a real bear appears holding Eduardito's lost teddy and looking for his own. The bear drops Eduardito's teddy and grabs his own, and they return to their own beds with their very own teddy bears. (themes: cooperation, problem-solving, feelings [fear])

📖 STORYPICKS

Margaret and Margarita, Margarita y Margaret by Lynn Reiser

El Tapiz de Abuela by Omar S. Castañeda, illustrated by Enrique O. Sánchez

ACTIVITIES

Game
Divide the group into pairs. Have them "teach" each other Spanish by using the flashcards they have made during the crafts activity. Periodically switch the cards around until every group has had every card.

Crafts
Encourage the children to create flash cards using index cards. On one side they can write or dictate a word and on the other side write that word in Spanish. If the children are below reading age, they can also use pictures on the cards. (If children in your group speak Spanish, they can be the "teachers.")

Outside
Play a version of *¿Donde Esta Mi Osito?* Hide a teddy bear outside, and work together to find the "osito."

SHOW NUMBER
212

Guest Readers

Brett Butler

Summary

Lucy is wrapping a present for Kino's mother. Kino forgot it was her birthday, and he can't afford to get her a nice present. Lucy reads a story about a little girl who makes a flower garden in a window box for her mother. This gives Kino an idea — he'll make something for his mother. He can paint her a picture. He starts work while Brett comes to read a story about a messy room. Kino gets frustrated because the letters he is painting are blending with the background. Lucy suggests he paint the background and wait for the next story, about a boy who is scared of a squeak, before painting the letters. After the book, Kino finishes his picture, and they discuss how it is better to stop and think before doing something.

 ## BOOKS READ

Flower Garden by Eve Bunting, illustrated by Kathryn Hewitt: A little girl and her father take a special trip to the grocery store to buy flowers for her mother's birthday. They carry them home on the bus and plant them in the window box. When she arrives, the mother is thrilled to have a beautiful flower garden in their city home. (themes: family, sharing, nature)

When the Fly Flew In by Lisa Westberg Peters, pictures by Brad Sneed: A little boy has a very messy room. He can't clean it because all the animals are asleep. Then a fly buzzes in and wakes the dog, which sets off a chain of events involving different animals who help him clean his room. (themes: imagination, animals, problem-solving, sequence of events)**

Nathaniel Willy, Scared Silly by Judith Mathews and Fay Robinson, illustrated by Alexi Natchev: Nathaniel Willy lives with his grandma in a little house in the country. One night the squeak in his bedroom door grows louder, and Nathaniel Willy is too scared to go to sleep. His Grandma brings different animals to help, but it is the wise woman down the road who oils the hinges so that Nathaniel Willy can go to sleep. (themes: family [grandmother], feelings [fear], problem-solving, animals)

 ## STORYPICKS

Just a Little Bit by Ann Tompert, illustrated by Lynn Munsinger

A Bicycle for Rosaura by Daniel Barbot, illustrated by Morella Fuenmayor

ACTIVITIES

Game
Make a cleanup game in the style of *When the Fly Flew In*. Each child can take on the role of an animal and use paws, wings, and hooves to clean up the mess.

Crafts
To prepare for this activity, draw a picture of the wise woman from *Nathaniel Willy, Scared Silly*, and make enough copies of it for everyone. On a big poster board, ask each child to draw an empty room with a scared child laying in bed. Have the children draw or color animals and then cut them out. As in *Nathaniel Willy, Scared Silly*, ask the children to place their animals in the room one at a time, until the "room" is packed with critters. Then they can color and cut out the wise woman drawing and place her in the room as well.

Outside
Take a walk through the neighborhood to look for flowers. Try a flower shop, a supermarket, or a park. Things to think about include the color and smell of the flowers, how much sunlight they get, and who waters them.

SHOW NUMBER 213

Summary

Guest Readers

Kathleen Quinlan

It's raining outside, so Kino and Mike have been playing inside all day. The Storyplace is a mess, and they are getting tired of games. Lucy suggests a story that asks what you would rather do. Kathleen comes for a visit to read a story about another kind of mess. Afterward, Kino and Mike clean up the Storyplace, and they read another story, about a girl who loves her dog.

 **BOOKS READ**

Would You Rather by John Burningham: This picture book presents a variety of different choices, some good and some bad, about what the reader would rather do, or have, or be. (themes: rhyme, problem-solving [making choices])

Pigs Aplenty, Pigs Galore! by David McPhail: A man is reading in bed one night when he hears the sound of munching. He finds pigs everywhere, eating and eating and munching away. When a pizza is delivered and the man gets the bill, he kicks the pigs out. They beg him to let them stay, so he relents and makes them clean everything up before he gets back into bed. (themes: rhyme, fantasy)

Boodil, My Dog by Pija Lindenbaum: A little girl describes the many ways that she loves her dog Boodil, whom no one else seems to appreciate in quite the same way. Boodil is not your typical dog — he walks slowly down the stairs, insists on going his own way home even though it takes longer, likes to look at bugs instead of chasing and fetching, and doesn't want to play with other dogs. Yet the little girl loves him just the way he is and thinks he is the best dog there is. (themes: friendship, uniqueness, animals)

 **STORYPICKS**

Muddigush by Kimberley Knutson

June 29, 1999 by David Wiesner

ACTIVITIES

Game
Play a choice game. Brainstorm and create a list with the group of things you all like to do and things you all have to do. Put each item on an individual index card, and place the cards all into a hat. Let each person pick two at random and choose the one he or she would rather do.

Crafts
For a snack, let the children create their own English muffin pizzas. Present the kids with tomato sauce, grated cheese, and English muffin halves. Let them create their own pizzas. To provide additional choices, you can offer other toppings like broccoli, mushrooms, or pepperoni. They can be eaten as is or baked.

Outside
Have the theme for outside play be pretending to be Boodil the dog. Encourage the children to try different roles, such as the dog, the owner, a veterinarian, or a pet shop owner.

Summary

Guest Readers

Angela Bassett

Kino is playing astronaut. When he grows up, that's what he wants to be. Now he is making a time capsule so people in the future can see what his world is like. Mara suggests that he include music. She sings the words of a book that is an illustrated version of an old song. They decide to put the book and a tape of the song into the capsule. Then Angela comes in with some kids to read. When she hears of Kino's dream to be an astronaut, she reads a book about a man who worked hard to make his dream come true. Afterward, she reads a poem about a little girl who wants to win the Nobel Prize.

 # BOOKS READ

Frog Went A-Courtin' retold by John Langstaff, pictures by Feodor Rojankovsky: This illustrated version of an old song tells the story of a frog who courts Miss Mouse and must get Uncle Rat's consent. He is asked about the wedding feast, which will take place at a tree where they will serve green beans and black-eyed peas. The uncle gives his consent, the animals bring things for the wedding feast, and a cat comes to break up the celebration. The honeymoon is spent in Paris, France. (themes: rhyme, music)

Uncle Jed's Barbershop by Margaree King Mitchell, illustrated by James Ransome: A little girl tells the story of her Uncle Jed, the only black barber in the county, who travels from town to town giving haircuts and dreaming of owning a barbershop of his own one day. Uncle Jed saves his money but loses his life savings twice. He finally opens his shop on his seventy-ninth birthday. Uncle Jed dies soon after the shop opens, but he has taught his niece how to achieve a dream. (themes: determination, family, self-esteem, feelings [disappointment, love])

Stories to Tell from **Meet Danitra Brown** by Nikki Grimes, illustrated by Floyd Cooper: In a poem, a little girl admires her friend Danitra, who wants to win the Nobel Prize. Her friend knows she'll do it. (themes: friendship, self-esteem)

STORYPICKS

Aunt Flossie's Hats (and Crab Cakes Later) by Elizabeth Fitzgerald Howard, paintings by James Ransome

The Hippopotamus Song by Michael Flanders and Donald Swann, illustrated by Nadine Bernard Westcott

ACTIVITIES

Game
Play a dream game. Have the kids close their eyes, and ask them to try to imagine or dream what they will be like as grown-ups. Let each share his or her "vision" with the class. Encourage everyone to ask questions of each other.

Crafts
Create "before" and "after" haircut pictures. The children can use string, yarn, or crayons to show their hair before and after a haircut.

Outside
In honor of Uncle Jed, ask everyone to use their imaginations and the normal outside resources to build a mock barbershop. Once the shop has been constructed they can take turns "cutting" each other's hair with their fingers. It will be important for the "customer" to communicate with the "stylist."

SHOW NUMBER 215

Summary

Guest Readers

Barry Corbin

Kino's friends are playing baseball outside, but he doesn't want to play along — he wants to be a cowboy. Mara discovers that Kino is really frustrated because he doesn't play baseball very well. She points out that it takes time and practice to be good at something. She sings the words of a book about a little boy who doesn't play baseball very well. Back at the Storyplace, they meet Barry, who has come with some cowboy books to read to Kino. He is dressed like a cowboy, shows them how to lasso, and passes out cowboy hats for everyone. He reads two stories, one about some cowboy villains and one about a girl who tries to catch a cow. Kino realizes that he, too, needs to keep at it and decides to give baseball another try.

 ## BOOKS READ

Playing Right Field by Willy Welch, illustrated by Marc Simont: A little boy who is always picked last for baseball thinks that he is just no good. He sits out in right field as the game goes on and daydreams without knowing the score. Then, suddenly, he notices that everyone is looking at him. As they point to the sky, a baseball falls into the boy's glove. He can play baseball after all. (themes: self-esteem, cooperation, rhyme)

Pug, Slug and Doug the Thug by Carol Saller, illustrated by Vicki Jo Redenbaugh: A dog, a cat, and a boy meet in front of a saloon as the sheriff posts a "wanted" poster for three bad guys, Pug, Slug and Doug the Thug. When the bad guys show up, there is a showdown at the saloon. The boy spits the straw in his mouth up to the chandelier, starting a fire that falls on a card game. Someone uses a barrel of pickle brine to put it out. The barrel knocks over a bucket of soapy water, the gang slips all over the floor, two are knocked down, and the boy ropes Doug the Thug. (themes: sequence of events, resourcefulness)

Hunting the White Cow by Tres Seymour, pictures by Wendy Anderson Halperin: When the white cow runs away from the barn to hide in the tobacco patch, no one can bring her back. Daddy goes out to get her, thinking it will be quickly done, but he is gone for a very long time. He goes out again, with help from the other men. He is gone even longer, and they still return without the cow. The little girl wants to go along but the men refuse to let her come. Even Grandpa, who is the best cow caller in the area, cannot seem to bring back the cow. One day the little girl sees the cow alone in the field. She leads it to the edge of the woods, where the cow refuses to go any further. The girl falls asleep while waiting. When her Daddy finds her, the cow is gone and the rope is broken. Using the rope as a belt, she dreams of the day she will get the cow on her own. (themes: problem-solving, cooperation)

STORYPICKS

The Field Beyond the Outfield by Mark Teague

The Cowboy and the Black-Eyed Pea by Tony Johnston, illustrated by Warren Ludwig

ACTIVITIES

Game
Hide a picture of a cow somewhere in the room. Provide clues to where it is. As in *Hunting the White Cow*, it will take a group effort to find the lost animal.

Crafts
Divide an 8.5" x 11" piece of paper into six rectangles, and draw the outline of a simple baseball card. Include a space for a photo and a place for the player's name below it. Cut out the individual baseball cards. Using the cards as frames, let the children create their own personal baseball cards by writing in their names and drawing pictures of themselves. To make the cards last longer, use heavy-weight construction paper or poster board.

Outside
Play catch using a foam football. This is best done between a child and an adult, one at a time, with a Nerf football. If the ball is thrown right at the child's chest, all he or she needs to do is hold the ball toward the body. This is a fun and easy way for younger children to develop confidence in their ability to catch a ball.

SHOW NUMBER 216

Summary

Guest Readers

Melissa Joan Hart

Martin Mull

Melissa, Kino and the kids are outside at a picnic table, talking about friends. Melissa reads a book about a girl who is chased by a crowd. Kino tells about a contest he is in with his friend Kevin to find out who can read the best story. Back at the Storyplace, Kino argues with Kevin about who is the winner of their contest. Martin and Lucy intervene by explaining that a contest can get in the way of a friendship. To help them understand, Martin reads a book about a contest between two friends that leads to potentially disastrous results. Afterward, the boys realize that being friends is more important than a contest and decide to read the last book together. They make a great story-reading team.

 **BOOKS READ**

Donna O'Neeshuck Was Chased by Some Cows by Bill Grossman, illustrated by Sue Truesdell: Donna O'Neeshuck gives a cow a pat on the head and finds herself being chased by the cow and her friends. Along the way, others join in the chase, all enjoying Donna's pats on the head. (themes: adventure, rhyme, sequence of events)

Don't Fidget a Feather by Erica Silverman, illustrated by S. D. Schindler: Duck and Gander are friends, but they can't seem to stop competing with each other. In the championship "freeze-in-place contest," in spite of many distractions, neither of them moves, until Duck saves Gander from a fox who is about to put him in a stew. To celebrate, they finish Fox's delicious vegetable stew. (theme: friendship)

Nothing at All by Denys Cazet: In the farmyard, the rooster crows, the horse wakes up, and the cow gets up in a very bad mood. As all the animals wake up, the scarecrow says nothing at all until a mouse gets into his pants. He wriggles and flips across the field, breaking into several pieces. The other animals rush to put him together and ask about breakfast. (themes: interactive story, animals, sounds)**

 **STORYPICKS**

The Most Wonderful Egg in the World by Helme Heine

Easy to See Why by Fred Gwynne

ACTIVITIES

Game

Play a *Don't Fidget* game. Have half the group move around to the sound of music. When the music stops, the children must freeze. At that point, the other children come in as animals and try to distract their frozen friends and get them to move without touching them. After the first round, have the children switch roles.

Crafts

Create a scarecrow. Cut out a human figure about six feet tall. Mount it onto cardboard, and have the kids draw on it and decorate it with vibrant and bright colors. After they have finished and it has dried, hang it on a wall. You can also attach it to a wooden post and stick it into the ground.

Outside

Have the children play a game of tag based on *Donna O'Neeshuck Was Chased by Some Cows*. One child starts off as Donna, and the rest are frozen. As she taps each one, he or she comes to life and joins in the chase.

Storytime

SHOW NUMBER 217

Summary

The episode begins with Kino questioning the feelings of nonhumans: Does eating a carrot hurt the carrot? Is a watered plant happy? He knows his dog likes to be played with and is sad when playtime is over. Lucy then sings the story of "Fairy Went A-Marketing." David Keith arrives with two friends to read a story about a man's feelings. The children discuss what makes them happy or sad and act out these moods with facial expressions. A last book is read about animals who share and compromise.

Guest Readers

David Keith

 **BOOKS READ**

Fairy Went A-Marketing by Rose Fyleman, illustrated by Jamichael Henterly: The story is about a series of trips that a young fairy makes to the market. On different trips she buys a fish in a bowl, a bird in a cage, and a mouse in a basket. In the end she lets them all go. (theme: feelings [generosity])

The Man Who Kept His Heart in a Bucket by Sonia Levitin, illustrated by Jerry Pinkney: A man who carries his broken heart in a bucket feels nothing when he eats pie, hears music, and sees a baby. Then, a lovely maiden steals his heart and will only return it when he solves the riddle of three golden scales. He sees a scale at the baker, where this time the pie warms his heart; he identifies the musical scales that this time inspire him to dance; and he recognizes the scales on the fish being carried by the father of a baby, whom he wants for his own. As he solves the riddle, he realizes his heart is in the right place and marries the beautiful maiden. (themes: feelings [love], friendship, fairy tale)

Mole's Hill by Lois Ehlert: The mole lives in his hill next to the water. The fox and raccoon ask the mole to move the hill so that they can go straight to the water. Instead of moving it, the mole makes the hill much bigger, plants flowers on it, and digs a tunnel for the other animals. In the end all of the animals are happy. (themes: sharing, problem-solving, animals, cooperation)

 **STORYPICKS**

Kinda Blue by Ann Grifalconi

Rabbit's Good News by Ruth Lercher Bornstein

ACTIVITIES

Game

Play a game of "guess the mood." Whisper the name of a feeling into the ear of the first player. The person will then act it out for the rest of the group to guess. Let each person have a turn. Try to use as many different emotions as possible.

Crafts

Help the children create fish like the one with the golden scales in *The Man Who Kept His Heart in a Bucket*. After the fish are completed, have the children trace them and cut out a slightly bigger fish. Glue or staple the different sizes together with some scrap paper in between to create puffy three-dimensional fish.

Outside

Cultivate caterpillars into butterflies. The caterpillars are available through a science department or pet store. After a week or so the caterpillars will have transformed into cocoons and then butterflies. Once they are butterflies, have a celebration outside where they are set free.

SHOW NUMBER 218

Summary

Guest Readers

James McDaniel

Kino is very distressed today because his mother told him that she will no longer be driving him to school. School is eight whole blocks away. He's a little worried because his mom won't be there. James reads a story about a bear who also has to learn to survive without his mother. Then he reads another story, about a little girl who finds herself lost in the African bush with a baby elephant. Kino is starting to feel better. The next day, Kino arrives very proud because he walked to school alone and liked it. Lucy reads him a story about a bear.

BOOKS READ

Bear by John Shoenherr: A little bear wakes up to find his mother's scent weak and her spot next to him cold. His mother is gone. He sadly sets out alone to look for food, without much success. He follows a trail, is chased by a moose, finds some sour berries, is chased by a larger bear, gets lost, and finally falls asleep. He wakes up hungrier than ever and stops for a drink at the stream. He falls in, only to discover plenty of salmon, which he eats to his heart's content. He grows bigger, his roar grows deeper, and he is soon able to chase other animals, even the other bears. He gradually forgets his mother and grows bigger than ever, ready for the winter. (themes: self-esteem, resourcefulness, animals, nature)

The Hunter by Paul Geraghty: Jemima sets out with her grandfather to collect honey. She plays at being a hunter but wanders too far and gets lost. She follows a mournful sound until she reaches a baby elephant crying over his mother, who has been killed by a group of hunters. She knows the baby will not survive alone in the bush, so she tries to lead the elephant back to his herd. She remembers that her parents told her that if she ever got lost she should follow the animals to the river at the end of the day, because her home is on the other side. A group of poachers passes them in the dark, and Jemima remembers that her parents told her to never lose hope. Then the elephants come, and she hands the baby over to them. Her mother later finds her sleeping by the river, and Jemima vows never to be a hunter. (themes: family, adventure, caring/concern for others, nature)

It's the Bear! by Jez Alborough: Eddie does not want to go into the forest for a picnic with his mother. He is afraid of the bear. When his mother realizes that she has forgotten the apple pie, she rushes back to get it, leaving Eddie alone in the woods. A big bear comes out while she is gone, and Eddie hides in the basket. The bear eats their picnic lunch, and, when he starts looking for desert, Eddie screams. His mother returns with the pie and at first doesn't believe him. But when she turns around and sees the bear, they flee the forest, and the bear gets his dessert after all. (themes: feelings [fear], rhyme)**

STORYPICKS

Cora and the Elephants by Lissa Rovetch, art by Lissa Rovetch and Martha Weston

Feliciana Feydra Le Roux by Tynia Thomassie, illustrated by Cat Bowman Smith

ACTIVITIES

Game
Play a game called "If I were a parent." Give all the children a turn to express one thing that they would do just like their parents do.

Crafts
Help the children make paper bag bear puppets. The kids will color bear teeth onto the mouths and add all the other features to the tops of the bags. After the puppets are finished, help the kids create a puppet show where the bears interact with each other.

Outside
Have a snack outside with a picnic theme. Before embarking on the picnic, assign every child a helping job. Create a list of things that need to be done, and then seek volunteers to do them.

SHOW NUMBER 219

Summary

Guest Readers

Laura Dern

Kino, who is painting with Lucy, is almost finished with his finger painting. Lucy brings in the mail with a letter and picture from a boy named Tony. Lucy reads a story about an errand at the post office. After Kino cleans up, Laura reads a book about a little shepherd boy from the Southwest. They talk about how books, like letters, can take you to faraway and new places; but, to write letters and enjoy books, you need to know how to read. Laura reads a book about a little girl who doesn't know how to read.

📖 BOOKS READ

Hi! by Ann Herbert Scott, illustrated by Glo Coalson: Margarita and her mother wrap up a present for her grandmother and take it to the post office. When they get there, they find a long line, so they wait. Margarita says "Hi!" to the many different people in line, but no one answers her. Finally, when it is their turn, Margarita reaches the woman behind the window and says "Hi," very quietly. The woman responds with a very loud and resounding "Hi!" Finally someone responded, and Margarita cheerfully repeats her good-byes all the way out. (themes: interactive story, friendship)**

The Shepherd Boy by Kristine L. Franklin, illustrated by Jill Kastner: Ben lives with his family in the Southwest, where he cares for the sheep with help from his dogs. After school each day, he leads all fifty sheep across the mesa, through the canyon, to a secret spring where the green grass grows. Then one day, one little ewe lamb is missing, so the little boy goes back through the canyon, where he finds her in the old cave houses among the ancient paintings on the wall. He leads her back home, where they all stay safe and far away from the coyotes. (themes: responsibility, animals)

Amber on the Mountain by Tony Johnston, paintings by Robert Duncan: Amber lives high on the mountain, where there is little contact with the world below and where few people know how to read. Once a man came on a horse to teach the mountain people to read and write, but he left before winter came. Then another man comes with his wife and daughter to build a road, even though the mountain people tell him that building a road will be impossible. Amber befriends his daughter, Anna, who becomes determined to teach Amber to read. The reading is hard and frustrating work, but the girls patiently keep at it, and Amber learns how to read. Before Amber learns to write, the road is complete, and the visiting family leaves the mountain. Amber gets letters from Anna. After hard work and much practice, Amber teaches herself to write, and Anna is surprised and thrilled to get a letter from her. (themes: friendship, resourcefulness, determination)

📖 STORYPICKS

The Jolly Postman or Other People's Letters by Janet and Allan Ahlberg

Dear Bear by Joanna Harrison

ACTIVITIES

Game
Divide the group into pairs. Each player must teach the other person how to read or write one word. Even if the word is the person's name, the game gives each player the opportunity to be a teacher and to learn something new.

Crafts
Give the children a large cardboard box to transform into an ancient cave with cave paintings inside. The outside of the box can have a natural texture, but the inside walls can be covered with cave paintings using the example provided in *The Shepherd Boy*. The pictures can be drawn or cut from magazines.

Outside
Play the *Hi!* game like Margarita. Take a walk around your neighborhood, and have the kids greet everybody they see. After the walk is completed, have a discussion about what the children observed and how people reacted to their friendliness.

Summary

Guest Readers

Litefoot

Kino is in his very messy room trying to find his animal book to learn more about his chameleon. Lucy picks Kino up but he can't find his hat anywhere in the mess. When they arrive at the Storyplace, Litefoot is there with the kids to read a book that tries to explain why things are, and another about a lazy bear who learns to change his ways. Kino decides to change his ways by learning to be neater and cleaning his room, where everything has been picked up and he has found his hat and his book.

BOOKS READ

Owl Eyes by Frieda Gates, illustrated by Yoshi Miyake: Raweno, the master of all spirits, made the world and all that is in it. To make the woodland creatures, he molded them from clay and allowed each one to pick its own color. As Raweno works, Owl interrupts with his opinion about how the other animals should look. Raweno tries to ignore him and his annoying behavior. He asks the animal what color he would like to be, but Owl keeps changing his mind. Raweno makes him sit up in the tree until he can make up his mind. Owl continues to interrupt, so Raweno turns him around. When Owl turns his head to interrupt, Raweno pushes Owl's head down so he can't turn around, yanks his ears up so he learns to listen, widens his eyes so that he will learn to watch, and dips him in the mud so that he will be brown and no one will see him. Finally, because Raweno works only by day, he makes Owl work only by night so that he will never have to see him. (themes: fairy tale, animals)

Tops & Bottoms adapted and illustrated by Janet Stevens: Once there was a very lazy bear with lots of land and money. Nearby lived a poor hare who lost all of his land. With no food left for their children, Hare and his wife present lazy Bear with a deal. Hare will do all the work planting the fields while bear continues to sleep. They will split the profits. He gives Bear his choice between the tops and bottoms of the crop. Hare cleverly gives Bear his choice of tops or bottoms of different vegetables, keeping the better half in each case for himself. From then on, Bear never again sleeps through another season. Hare uses his profits to buy back his land and open a vegetable stand. The two live as neighbors but are never business partners again. (themes: resourcefulness, nature)

STORYPICKS

The Royal Nap by Charles C. Black, illustrated by James Stevenson

The Night of the Stars by Douglas Gutiérrez, illustrated by Maria Fernanda Oliver

ACTIVITIES

Game
In *Owl Eyes* the children heard a story about how the owl got its special features. Randomly assign one animal to each child, and have him or her make up a story about how it got the special qualities that it has.

Crafts
Give each child a piece of paper divided into halves. On one side the child will draw the owl as he was, and the on other he or she will draw what the owl became. This quiet activity can be done independently or while the children are listening to the story.

Outside
Visit a farmer's market or any store that sells fruits and vegetables. As a group, look at the different items, and think about whether the part that is eaten grew above or below the ground. Discuss what part of each fruit or vegetable is used and what part is not used.

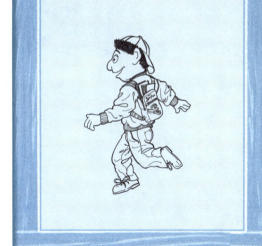

Storytime

SHOW NUMBER 221

Guest Readers

Joey Lawrence

Mara Wilson

Summary

Kino has joined a children's theater group but is contemplating quitting because he doesn't know any of the other children. Lucy encourages him to stay in the group by explaining that as he gets to know the other kids he'll be fine. Lucy reads a book about a lonely spider who makes friends, and then Mara reads a story about a dragon who doesn't fit in. Finally, Joey reads a story about a shy boy who is able to break out of his shell. The themes of friendship have inspired Kino to remain in the theater group.

 ## BOOKS READ

Miss Spider's Tea Party written and illustrated by David Kirk: In this counting book, Miss Spider sips her tea while watching other insects on the leaves and wishes they were her friends. One by one, ants, beetles, and bees turn down her invitations for tea, fearing that she'll catch them in her web and eat them. Then a moth accidentally falls into the web. Miss Spider helps the moth and then gives it tea. The moth tells all of the other insects what happened, and they then all go for a friendly tea with Miss Spider. (themes: friendship, rhyme, counting, feelings [loneliness])

Elvira by Margaret Shannon: Elvira is tormented by other dragons for not eating princesses or rolling in the mud. She wanders far away to where she finds some princesses. There she wears fancy dresses and makeup. Her parents show up and almost eat her, thinking she is a princess. They take her home, and all of the other dragons now want to be like Elvira. (themes: differences, uniqueness, identity)

Wilson Sat Alone by Debra Hess, illustrated by Diane Greenseid: At school, Wilson sits, eats, reads, and plays alone. A new girl comes to school alone on the first day, but she joins the other children after that. When she sees Wilson alone, she roars at him. To the surprise of everyone, he roars back and from then on Wilson is never alone. (theme: friendship)

We Could Be Friends from ***I Like You, If You Like Me*** by Myra Cohn Livingston: This short poem is about the things that friends do together. (theme: friendship)

 ## STORYPICKS

A Weekend with Wendell by Kevin Henkes

Matthew and Tilly by Rebecca C. Jones, illustrated by Beth Peck

ACTIVITIES

Game
Play a game of "Simon Says," giving everyone an opportunity to be the leader.

Crafts
On a large piece of white poster board, draw a huge spider web with a lonely spider in it. The kids will each create a bug, real or imagined, that is having tea. After they have been colored and cut out, the bugs will be placed on the web to create a huge, happy, and colorful tea party like Miss Spider had.

Outside
Play a game of *Wilson Sat Alone*. Assign a few kids to be the "shy" kids. The job of the other kids is to include the "shy" kids in group games and activities. The job of the shy kids is to try to communicate without words.

Summary

Guest Readers

John Astin

Elijah Wood

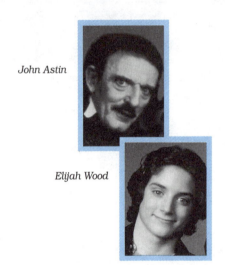

It is Halloween, and Kino is dressed as Count Dracula. He and Jenny, who is dressed as a pirate, arrive trick-or-treating at John's house. They find that he is dressed as Dracula too! After their treats, John offers them a story, but he needs to borrow a flashlight to sing the words of a story about Dracula's house. Afterward, Kino and Jenny head back to the Storyplace for Lucy's annual game of "scared silly." Lucy pops out of the shadows as a witch and demands that they answer her riddle or hand over some candy. Elijah jumps out of the story circle dressed as a werewolf and offers to read the next story, about a big pumpkin. Afterward, the kids head back into the dark and find Lucy stirring a big cauldron. She quizzes them with another riddle, and they hand over more candy. Out of her cauldron, she pulls another book and reads them the story of an old lady who isn't afraid of anything.

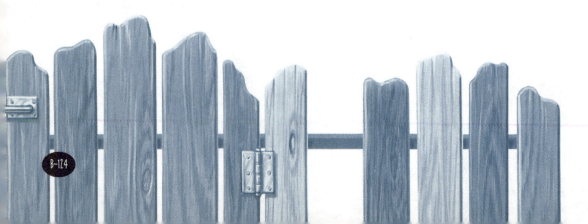

 **BOOKS READ**

The House That Drac Built by Judy Sierra, illustrated by Will Hillenbrand: In this Halloween version of the classic cumulative tale, a series of increasingly ghoulish characters encounter each other in Drac's haunted house, and things get a little out of hand. Then a group of trick-or-treating children knock on the door and set things straight — they frighten the fiend, zap the zombie, rewrap the mummy, close the coffin, shush the monster, soothe the manticore, cage the werewolf, pet the cat, and bandage the bat. (themes: holidays [Halloween], fantasy, feelings [fear], sequence of events)

The Big Pumpkin by Erica Silverman, illustrated by S. D. Schindler: Once there was a witch who wanted a pumpkin pie. So she planted a seed, and watered and weeded until it grew to be a very big pumpkin. But by Halloween night, the pumpkin is so big that no matter how hard she pulls and tugs, she cannot pull it from the vine. Though she wants the pumpkin for herself, she needs help, so she reluctantly lets first a ghost, then a vampire, and then a mummy try to pull that pumpkin out. But no matter how hard they pull and tug, nobody can pull that pumpkin out. Finally, a bat comes along and suggests they all pull together. The pumpkin comes out, the witch makes pie, and she shares it with her new friends. When they are gone she is so sorry, she plants a new seed to start over again. (themes: holidays [Halloween], fantasy, sharing, cooperation, friendship, problem-solving)

The Little Old Lady Who Was Not Afraid of Anything by Linda Williams, illustrated by Megan Lloyd: A little old lady who isn't afraid of anything goes for a walk to get some spices and herbs in the forest. But she is gone for so long that it gets dark before she gets home. Suddenly, in the dark path ahead, she sees things clomping, wiggling, shaking, and saying "boo." This sends her running all the way home. There is a knock on the door, and the scarecrow announces that he is there to scare her. When she tells him she isn't afraid of anything, he is very unhappy. But then the old lady thinks of something to make him feel better — she sets him out in the garden where he can be a scarecrow. (themes: holidays [Halloween], fantasy, feelings [fear, courage], resourcefulness, problem-solving)

Halloween Howls: Riddles That Are a Scream written and illustrated by Giulio Maestro: A variety of riddles revolving around the theme of Halloween. (themes: holidays [Halloween], rhymes [riddles])

 **STORYPICKS**

Granny Greenteeth and the Noise in the Night by Kenn and Joanne Compton, illustrated by Kenn Compton

A Job for Wittilda by Caralyn Buehner, illustrated by Mark Buehner

ACTIVITIES

Game
Just like *The Little Old Lady Who Was Not Afraid of Anything*, assemble body parts to make a scarecrow. On a large poster board, draw the outline of the scarecrow. On separate pieces of paper, cut out different body parts. Put these pieces together in a bag or a box decorated with Halloween decorations. Have people put their hands in and pull out a body part, which they should attach to the poster outline.

Crafts
Work together to make a pumpkin pie, just like the witch and her new friends in *The Big Pumpkin*. On poster board, take turns writing down the recipe by drawing pictures of the ingredients. Everyone can have a role in adding and mixing. Share the pie at a Halloween party.

Outside
Find a dark corner of the yard or park, and have the group make a haunted house, like *The House That Drac Built*. Using dark fabrics, toilet paper, and string, you can make scary corners and spider webs that people can crawl in and out of.

Summary

Guest Readers

Jane Seymour

Lucy and Kevin are drawing a family tree on a big piece of paper. Kino is interested to learn what a family tree is and remembers a book about a llama who doesn't know who her mother is. Lucy finds it on the shelf and reads it to the boys. Jane arrives at the story circle, and Kino tells her about Kevin's family tree. They talk about families, and Jane reads a book about the son of a Native American chief who gets carried away from his village. The group talks about families and Kevin puts up his tree on the storyboard. One small branch is for his Aunt Paula, who is small but smart. Lucy suggests that Jane read a book that a young friend has brought, a story about a monkey who is small but smart, too. Afterward, Kino is ready to start on his family tree.

BOOKS READ

Is Your Mama a Llama? by Deborah Guarino, illustrated by Steven Kellogg: A curious llama asks a series of friends, a bat, a signet, a calf, a seal, and a kangaroo, if their mothers are llamas. In rhyme, they respond with descriptions of their mamas, which encourage the llama and the reader to guess the answer on the next page. Finally he asks his friend Llyn, another llama, and learns that both of their mamas are llamas, from the same herd. (themes: rhyme, animals, identity, family [mother], interactive story)**

Storm Boy written and illustrated by Paul Owen Lewis: One day the chief's son goes out fishing alone and is lost in a storm. He finds himself under a new sky in a new village where everything is large. The villagers invite him in, offer him food, and teach him their dances. He in turn teaches them the songs and dances of his village. Soon, however, he begins to miss his home. The chief tells the boy to hold on to his staff and wish for home. The boy is carried home on a whale, and learns he has been gone a year. He tells his family about his trip. (themes: fantasy, differences, feelings [homesickness])

The Monkey and the Crocodile written and illustrated by Paul Galdone: A very hungry crocodile is determined to eat a quick monkey who lives in the mango tree above him. He offers the monkey a ride on his back to an island where the fruit is ripe. When the monkey realizes the crocodile intends to eat him, he tricks the crocodile into turning back to get the monkey's heart, which is the tastiest part. The monkey jumps safely back to land, laughs down at the crocodile, and moves on to new tree. The greedy crocodile tracks him down and lies waiting for him on a nearby rock. The monkey quickly spots him there and tricks the crocodile into opening his mouth wide, knowing that crocodiles close their eyes when they open their mouths. While the crocodile is opening his mouth, the monkey makes it back to the safety of his tree, and both animals agree to stay out of each other's way. (themes: feelings [greed], resourcefulness, animals)

STORYPICKS

It's Not My Turn to Look for Grandma by April Halprin Wayland, illustrated by George Booth

The Toll-Bridge Troll by Patricia Rae Wolff, illustrated by Kimberly Bulcken Root

ACTIVITIES

Game

Play "M Is for Monkey and C Is for Crocodile" and learn some new letters and sounds by having the children think up all the words they can that begin with M and then the ones that begin with C. Tally up at the end to see which letter begins the most words.

Crafts

Work together on making a "family and friends tree," like the one made by the kids at the Storyplace. Outline and cut the tree trunk and leaves out of brown and green colored paper and then glue them to a large sheet. In the leaves, draw pictures of family and friends. Afterward, individuals can describe some of these people to the rest of the group.

Outside

When the chief's son travels to a new village in *Storm Boy*, he encounters many new things. Take a walk around the neighborhood, and have people notice everything they see that makes it distinctive. When you come back ask everybody to draw a map of the trip.

SHOW NUMBER 303

Summary

Guest Readers

Victoria Rowell

Kino and Jenny are getting ready for the "Best of the Best Day" at school. Jenny is practicing with Victoria to be the best dancer, and Kino is practicing with Lucy to win the obstacle course. When Jenny asks Victoria how she learned to dance, she explains that her mother loved dancing. Victoria reads a book that reminds her of her mom. After the story, they talk about how important it is to practice to become good at something. Lucy reads a book about a girl who practiced hard to become a tightrope walker. Victoria points out that it is important to enjoy what you are practicing too. Jenny says she loves to dance, so Victoria reads a fun book that everyone can dance to.

BOOKS READ

My Mama Had a Dancing Heart by Libba Moore Gray, illustrated by Raul Colon: A little girl whose mother loves to dance describes how they dance together through the seasons of the year. In the spring, they dance in the fresh grass, then drink tea and read poems. In the summer, they dance on the shore, then drink lemonade and collect seashells. In the fall they dance among the falling leaves and press them in wax paper. In the winter, they make snow angels, dance like snowmen and drink hot cocoa with marshmallows. Now the girl has become a ballerina on the stage, and this was because her mother shared her dancing heart. (themes: family [mother], feelings [happiness], nature)

Mirette on the Highwire written and illustrated by Emily Arnold McCully: In the late nineteenth century, the Widow Gateau and her daughter Mirette run a boarding house in Paris for traveling players from all over the world. One day Mirette is inspired by Monsieur Bellini, a mysterious retired tightwire walker, to learn to walk the tightrope. He refuses to teach her, but is gradually won over by her determination and natural ability. Then an agent from London arrives and tells Mirette about Bellini's marvelous past feats. Mirette asks her teacher to join her on a tour, but Bellini confesses that he has retired because he is afraid. Mirette is so disappointed that Bellini and the agent come up with a plan for Bellini to try to perform again. But as he steps out on the wire, he freezes in fear. Mirette races to the roof on the other side of the rope and walks across to Bellini with open arms, encouraging him to walk towards her. The crowd roars, and the agent organizes a world tour for the new act. (themes: determination, caring/concern for others, friendship)

Twist with a Burger, Jitter with a Bug by Linda Lowery, illustrated by Pat Dypold: This colorful book celebrates dance as images and animals dance across the pages in a variety of exuberant ways. (themes: nature, music, fantasy, rhyme)

STORYPICKS

Wilma Unlimited by Kathleen Krull, illustrated by David Diaz

Little Bobo by Serena Romanelli, illustrated by Hans de Beer

ACTIVITIES

Game
Play a game of dance statues. Turn on some happy dancing music, and have everybody in the room dance around. Keep the tape player or music source hidden so that at random moments the music can be stopped. When the music stops, so should the dancers. Anyone who is caught moving during the silence is eliminated. The last one dancing is the winner.

Crafts
In *My Mama Had a Dancing Heart*, the girl and her mother dance through the year and watch the seasons change. Have people make a calendar by drawing pictures of the different seasons on the tops of twelve sheets of paper and then attaching them at the center in a booklet. Later, add the grid on the bottom halves of the paper, and fill in the dates.

Outside
Work together to put on a circus by taking on the parts of all the traveling players at the Widow Gateau's boarding house. Someone could pretend to be the tightrope walker, by laying string on the ground; someone could be the lion tamer; some can be clowns; someone could juggle; another could be a tumbler. Invite parents or friends to watch the circus when you are ready to perform.

SHOW NUMBER 304

Summary

Kino arrives at the Storyplace to find twins Tia and Tamara playing "mirror." They have brought a pile of books to the Storyplace and choose one to read together, about a wolf who tries to catch a pig who always manages to escape. The book reminds Kino that he has to be home early. Later, Kino wishes he had a twin to play with, too. That night he dreams that he has a twin named Snoozer, who loves to play with his dog. Kino suggests that Lucy read them a book about a very special dog. When Kino wakes up, he is sorry that the dream is over and Snoozer is gone. He heads to the Storyplace to tell Lucy, Freddy, and the kids about his dream. To cheer him up, Freddy reads a story about a little girl and her grandfather. Kino realizes his twin brother was like the story — he wasn't real, but he made Kino happy.

Guest Readers

Tia and Tamara Mowry

Freddy Fender

BOOKS READ

Suddenly! written and illustrated by Colin McNaughton: Preston the pig is walking home from school but doesn't know that a big, hungry wolf is following him. The wolf is about to pounce when suddenly Preston remembers that he was supposed to stop at the store and turns the other way. He is doing his shopping, with the wolf hanging over the aisle, when suddenly he remembers he left the money in his desk. In this way, Preston narrowly misses being eaten, and the wolf repeatedly lands in a bruised heap. Preston arrives home to his mother, whose shadow looks like the wolf, when suddenly she gives him a big hug. He has a funny feeling he was being followed all day. In the background, the wounded wolf is carried away on a stretcher. (themes: cause and effect, interactive story)

Courtney written and illustrated by John Burningham: When the kids plead for a dog, their parents give in but tell them to make sure they get one with a good pedigree. The kids pick Courtney, an old dog with unknown roots. The parents are very dubious about an unreliable mongrel, but it soon becomes clear that Courtney is no ordinary dog — he can cook, serve at the table, and play the violin, and he even saves the baby in a house fire. Then Courtney disappears. The children mourn, and their parents blame it on Courtney's bad pedigree. That summer the family takes a vacation, and, while boating, the children are cast adrift in the water without their oars. The parents stand on the beach helplessly until something pulls the boat back to the shore and the children are saved. No one knows who or what saved the children, but in the distance behind the family is the shadow of a dog in the hills. (themes: friendship, caring/concern for others, animals, differences)

The Gullywasher written and illustrated by Joyce Rossi: Letitia and her Abuelito are waiting for the gullywasher, a desert thundershower, to end so they can go on their walk. While they wait, Letitia asks her grandfather to tell her about when he was a vaquero, a cowboy. He tells her a series of tall tales about how he changed from being a young cowboy to the older man he is today. (themes: family [grandfather], fantasy, imagination, nature)

STORYPICKS

Medio Pollito, Half-Chicken by Alma Flor Ada, illustrated by Kim Howard

My Dog Rosie by Isabelle Harper, illustrated by Barry Moser

ACTIVITIES

Game

Designate one person to be Preston and everyone else wolves. Preston stands on one side of the room with his or her back turned to the wolves, who are lined up on the opposite side of the room. The objective of the wolves is to catch Preston. When Preston says "Go!" the wolves start sneaking behind. At random moments, Preston turns around quickly and says "Suddenly," and the wolves freeze. If Preston catches any of the wolves moving, they are out. If all the wolves are eliminated before they reach Preston, the pig wins. The first wolf to catch Preston is the winner.

Crafts

In *Courtney*, a special dog is able to do many things that humans can do. Ask everyone to draw pictures of all the things that real dogs use, like a bowl, a bone, a ball, or a leash.

Outside

Organize a trip to a retirement home, or invite an older friend to visit. Encourage people to ask questions about the past and to learn what life was like before they were born. Make some comparisons about how things are different.

Guest Readers

Dennis Haskins

Summary

Kino is looking all over his room for a puzzle game. When he heads over to the Storyplace, he explains to Dennis that today is trade day at school. He has been assigned to trade something with John, but he is having a hard time thinking of what to trade because he and John are like opposites. Dennis suggests reading a story about a contrary mouse. Lucy comes in with John and the kids. John has brought some books to leave at the Storyplace, and Dennis reads one from Ethiopia. Meanwhile, Kino's curiosity is piqued because John has brought a big box for trade day and is asking Lucy to borrow some mysterious supplies. To distract him, Dennis suggests that Kino read the next story, about a cat who borrows things from her friends. Everyone talks about how the animals shared with the cat, and John announces he is ready for his trade. John knows how much Kino loves cars, so he has built him a racetrack from things he has found around the house. Kino knows how much John likes math, so he presents him with a Rubik's cube.

 **BOOKS READ**

Contrary Mary written and illustrated by Anita Jeram: One morning, Mary the mouse wakes up feeling contrary. All day long, she decides to do the opposite of what she is supposed to. She dresses backward, asks for dinner at breakfast, and walks on her hands. That night her mother tucks Contrary Mary in her bed upside down, kisses her toes, and says good morning. Contrary Mary laughs and laughs, giving her Contrary Mom a big hug. (themes: cooperation, family [mother], feelings [love], opposites) **

The Perfect Orange: A Tale from Ethiopia by Frank P. Araujo, Ph.D., illustrated by Xiao Jun Li: In the mountains of Ethiopia lives an orphan girl named Tshai, who gives a beautiful, perfect orange she finds to her ruler, the great Nigus. Along the way, she passes the big house of Ato Jib, the Lord Hyena, who offers to trade the orange for a gourd to carry water. Tshai refuses and presents the orange to the Nigus, who offers to give her a purse of gold and a casket of jewels in return. Tshai refuses them both and starts for her home. Nigus sends the royal chamberlain after her with a donkey loaded with his gifts of wealth. She accepts the donkey. The hyena is so impressed by her trade with the ruler that he offers all of his lands and his cattle to the great Nigus, who accepts his gifts and offers his most prized possession, the perfect orange, in return. When Tshai returns home, her neighbors discover the gifts from the Great Nigus and together they celebrate her good fortune. (themes: feelings [generosity, greed], caring/concern for others, sharing, fairy tale)

This and That by Jules Sykes, illustrated by Tanya Linch: Down on the farm, Cat wakes up early to start her busy, special day. She borrows something from each animal — a stable, straw, hay, wool, feathers, hair, and a lovely purple ribbon. The animals are glad to share with Cat, but they want to know what she is up to. "This and that," she answers when they ask. Overcome by curiosity, the animals follow Cat into the stable, where they find two new kittens in a nest made from the things she borrowed. Cat wonders what to name her children, and the animals suggest she call them "This" and "That." (themes: friendship, sharing, feelings [generosity], animals, resourcefulness, interactive story) **

STORYPICKS

Sam and the Lucky Money by Karen Chinn, illustrated by Cornelius Van Wright and Ying-Hwa Hu

Lucy's Picture by Nicola Moon, pictures by Alex Ayliffe

ACTIVITIES

Game
Present the group with a large orange, and ask everyone to gather on the floor in a circle. Pass the orange around, and ask each person to take a turn holding it. The person with the orange should describe for the group the present he or she would most like to give. Afterward, cut up the orange, and give everyone a piece.

Crafts
Make opposite puzzle pairs by having people draw two opposites on separate sides of a piece of paper. Glue them to a piece of cardboard and then cut a crooked or curved line between the images. These can be used as a puzzle to match the opposite pairs.

Outside
In *Contrary Mary*, a contrary mouse wakes up one morning and decides to do everything the opposite way. Go outside, identify objects around you, and ask children to suggest their opposites. Examples might be sky and earth, sun and rain.

SHOW NUMBER 306

Summary

Kino is having trouble starting a story for school, so Lucy suggests that he investigate how authors come up with their stories. Patricia Polacco explains that she gets her story ideas from experiences she had as a girl or stories told to her by her grandmother, and then she reads a book she wrote that takes place in Russia. Kino investigates at the library, where he meets James, who reads a story about a pet dog. Back at the Storyplace, Kino finds author/illustrator Peter Catalanotto, who reads a story he wrote about his family, told through his daughter's eyes. Now Kino thinks it will be easier to write his story — he will think about things that really happened to him, and he will use his imagination, too!

Guest Readers

Peter Catalonotto

James Avery

B-134

 **BOOKS READ**

Babushka Baba Yaga written and illustrated by Patricia Polacco: Baba Yaga is a lonely creature in the forest, feared by the people of the local village. She longs for a grandchild of her own to love, like the babushkas from the village. One day, she dresses up like a babushka and is welcomed in the village. Natasha and her son Victor have no Babushka, and Baba Yaga offers to help. Everyone is happy until the day that the babushkas tell Victor frightening stories about the horrible Baba Yaga. Baba Yaga leaves in the night before Victor can find out who she is. But Victor misses her and goes to look for her at the edge of the forest, where he is surrounded by wolves. The townspeople watch in horror as Baba Yaga emerges from the forest and saves him from the wolves. There is a big celebration, and from then on she is known as Babushka Baba Yaga. (themes: family [grandmother], feelings [loneliness], friendship, caring/concern for others, differences, fairy tale)

The Old Dog by Charlotte Zolotow, illustrated by James Ransome: One morning, Ben comes downstairs to pet his dog, but the animal doesn't move — he doesn't even wag his tail or open his eyes. Ben's father explains that the dog is dead; he was an old dog. After school, the dog is not there to watch Ben drink his milk or play outside. Ben misses his dog so much he cries. And there is no dog there to comfort him or to see the new dog his father is bringing home. (themes: animals, feelings [sadness], friendship)

The Painter written and illustrated by Peter Catalanotto: A little girl describes a day in her life with her father, who is a painter. Every morning they have breakfast and lunch together, and the girl asks her father to do different things with her, but he says "Not yet," and heads up to paint in his studio, where she is not allowed. After dinner one day, they do magic tricks and when she asks him to read a book or play with puppets, he says no. Tonight they will paint in his studio! When her mother admires her work and tells her she will be a painter too when she grows up, the girl assures her that she already is. (themes: family [father], sharing)

STORYPICKS

A Story, A Story retold and illustrated by Gail E. Haley

Booby Hatch written and illustrated by Betsy Lewin

ACTIVITIES

Game
Just as Kino is writing a story for school, have people collaborate together on a story. Go around a circle, and ask each person to contribute a sentence until everyone has had a turn and the story has an end.

Crafts
Create an art gallery in the classroom or in the home. Organize a variety of art projects in different media, such as drawing, painting, collage, papier mache, play-doh sculpture, etc. Display and arrange the artwork, and have the group collaborate on an invitation or announcement inviting parents, friends, and neighbors to come to see the art at an "opening."

Outside
Take a trip to an art museum, if possible, or a local library or bookstore to look at photographs of paintings by famous artists.

Summary

Guest Readers

Janeane Garofalo

Kino is playing checkers with his new friend John, who admits that he played with an imaginary friend until he met Kino. This reminds Kino of a book about a girl with a pretend friend, which Janeane reads. Afterward, it's time for Lucy to take Kino to the dentist. Kino acknowledges that he is a little scared, so John offers to come along. Lucy suggests they bring a book. In the waiting room, Lucy reads about a scary monster who turns out to be not so scary after all. Back at the Storyplace, Kino looks for a new book to read and Lucy reports to Janeane that he was very brave at the dentist. Janeane reads a book about a rabbit with big ears who doesn't listen well.

 **BOOKS READ**

Jessica written and illustrated by Kevin Henkes: Ruthie has an imaginary friend named Jessica. Ruthie's parents tell her there is no Jessica, but Ruthie knows there is. They do everything together. When Ruthie starts kindergarten, her parents suggest that Jessica stay home, but Jessica goes anyway. Then a little girl comes up to Ruthie and asks to be her partner. Ruthie doesn't know how to answer until the girl says her name is Jessica. (themes: friendship, imagination, family)

I'm Coming to Get You! written and illustrated by Tony Ross: A spaceship is rushing toward a small planet. Out jumps a loathsome monster who does terrible things there. Then he sees the pretty blue planet Earth and picks up little Tommy Brown at bedtime, listening to monster stories, on his radar screen. As Tommy checks the house for monsters before getting into bed, the monster in the spaceship tracks him down and waits for morning to attack. In the morning, Tommy is on his way to school when the monster roars and pounces but he is only the size of a bug and Tommy walks on by. (themes: feelings [fear, relief], fantasy, size)

Listen, Buddy by Helen Lester, illustrated by Lynn Munsinger: Buddy is a rabbit with big beautiful ears who does not listen. He brings wash instead of squash and a hen instead of a pen and slices his bed instead of the bread. One day, they give Buddy permission to go for a long hop and warn him to be careful of the Scruffy Varmint. As usual, Buddy doesn't listen and ends up at the Scruffy Varmint's cave, where he is making some soup. Buddy offers to help, but he does all the wrong things. The Varmint loses his temper and threatens to put Buddy in his soup. This time Buddy listens and hops very fast all the way home. From then on, Buddy listens. (themes: responsibility, cooperation)

STORYPICKS

Custard the Dragon and the Wicked Knight by Ogden Nash, illustrated by Lynn Munsinger

Rebel written and illustrated by John Schoenherr

ACTIVITIES

Game

Play a game of telephone, and see if people can listen any better than Buddy the rabbit. Gather the group in a circle, and select one person who will make up a phrase and whisper it in the ear of the person sitting at his or her side. This person then whispers the phrase in the ear of the next. This continues around the circle until it reaches the last one. The first person should announce what the original phrase was and the last should announce what it has become. This can be repeated until everyone has had a turn to make up a phrase.

Crafts

Learn about the concept of comparative size by drawing a chart with three columns on a poster board. At the top of each column, draw gradually larger monsters. Have people draw their own monsters on one of three sizes of index cards. Afterward, they should bring their monster up and match it to the correct column.

Outside

Who can see Jessica? Hide a doll somewhere outside and have people divide into pairs to go find her. Pairs should remain together by holding hands at all times.

Summary

Guest Readers

Joseph Marcel

Kino is building a skyscraper of blocks when a bug starts buzzing around his head. As he tries to swat it, he accidentally knocks down his tower. Lucy comes in with Lily and Joseph to read a book, followed by Kino who is swatting at the bug with a badminton racket. Joseph suggests that Kino might like the bug in his story better and he reads a book about a bug who gets swallowed by a boy. Afterward they talk about bugs that are germs, and everyone tries again to get rid of the bug. Joseph reads another book, about a dog who is bothered by fleas. After the story, the bug is back and Kino heads home, hoping to get rid of the bug. Back at the Storyplace the next day, the bug returns while they are rebuilding the block tower. They pretend the bug is gone, and Lucy reads a book about using your imagination. Then she sings a rap poem about a bug. When Kino recites another bug poem, his bug comes back. He tries to defend himself by taping a strainer to his body but ends up a sticky ball of tape.

 **BOOKS READ**

Buz written and illustrated by Richard Egielski: Buz, a fly, gets eaten with a spoonful of cornflakes by a young boy. He tries to escape but goes the wrong way and gets stuck in the boy's eye. The doctor gives the boy some pills, who head into his mouth to track Buz down. He manages to escape but when he emerges from his hiding place, they catch him again, as water begins to well up into the boy's head — he is in the bath. Buz swims away and arrives home tired and wet. His doctor examines him and determines that he has caught a germ. (themes: adventure, fantasy)

A Flea in the Ear by Stephen Wyllie, illustrated by Ken Brown: A dog who is pestered by fleas is guarding the hens in the farmyard one night when a hungry fox tries to make a deal for the hens. The dog refuses but is tricked by the fox into trying to drown the fleas in the pond. The fleas beg the dog to spare them and promise never to bother him again. When the dog returns home, he finds that the fox has taken his hens. He tells the fox that the drowning didn't work because the pond was full of fat, juicy ducks. The greedy fox races off to the pond, where the fleas jump all over him, and the dog rescues his stolen hens. (themes: animals, problem-solving, responsibility)

If written and illustrated by Sarah Perry: This colorful picture book depicts, in a series of humorous drawings, all sorts of fantasy scenarios — if cats could fly and if frogs ate rainbows. At the end, the book encourages the reader to think up some more. (themes: imagination, fantasy)

 **STORYPICKS**

Insects Are My Life by Megan McDonald, pictures by Paul Brett Johnson

Why Mosquitoes Buzz in People's Ears by Verna Aardema, pictures by Leo and Diane Dillon

ACTIVITIES

Game

Play an imagination game, inspired by *If*. Give players instructions of things they must do in unusual ways. For example, ask people to cross the room without walking, or ask them to clap without using their hands. Afterward, compare the different and creative things people did.

Crafts

Ask the children to make their own animals that have fleas. Make cut-outs of a fox and a dog, using colored paper, and give one pair to each child. Use a three-hole punch with black construction paper to make a collection of fleas that the children can glue onto their animals. They could also draw the fleas on with markers or crayons.

Outside

Launch a scientific expedition to search for bugs. Check inside cracks, under rocks, and in trees and bushes, for all the different types of insects in your neighborhood. When you return, ask each person to draw a picture of a bug. Organize a chart with all the different kinds of bugs that were found.

Guest Readers

Michael Horse

Summary

Marcus and Kino are watching Lucy photograph plants and animals. Marcus suggests they make this "Animal Day" — they can read animal books, eat animal crackers, and make animal sounds. Lucy reads a book about pretend animals. Then Kino is squirted by a skunk and he smells terrible. Back at the story circle, Lucy is working on her photo album with Marcus when Kino returns in clean clothes. Michael arrives to read a story and notices that something still smells. He reads a book about how the tortoise got his shell. Everyone tries to make an animal noise. Marcus suggests that they read a book about real animals this time, and he reads one about a bear and her cub. Afterward, everyone can still smell Kino's skunk, so he heads home to triple-wash his clothes.

 **BOOKS READ**

The Little Mouse, the Red Ripe Strawberry and the Big Hungry Bear by Don and Audrey Wood, illustrated by Don Wood: A little mouse finds a big ripe strawberry and is about to pick it when the narrator warns the mouse about the big hungry bear who can smell ripe strawberries from a mile away, especially if they are just picked. The mouse picks the strawberry but decides that the only way to save the strawberry is to cut it in half and share it with the narrator. (themes: sharing, feelings [fear])

The Leopard's Drum retold and illustrated by Jessica Souhami: Osebo makes a magnificent new drum that is the envy of all the animals. Everyone wants the drum — even Nyame, the Sky God. But Osebo is too proud and refuses to share his drum with anyone, even a powerful god. Nyame offers a reward to the animal who can bring the drum to him. Only Achicheri, the little tortoise with a soft shell, is able to trick Osebo into crawling into his drum, which he pushes to the Sky God. The god is so grateful that he presents the tortoise with a new, hard shell to protect her from fierce animals. (themes: fairy tale, sharing, animals, resourcefulness, problem-solving)

Honey Paw and Lightfoot by Jonathan London, illustrated by Jon Van Zyle: In June, two grizzly bears, Honeypaw and Old Man, mate and then go their own ways. Through the winter Honeypaw hibernates until her cub, Lightfoot, is born. She nurses him in the den until spring arrives and it is time to emerge. Together they hunt, graze, play, and defend themselves against the Big Hairy One, who wounds Honeypaw as she tries to defend Lightfoot. As Honeypaw's wounds heal, they are able to play and hunt again. Soon Lightfoot will be ready to go off on his own. (themes: animals, family [mother], resourcefulness, nature)

STORYPICKS

The Night I Followed the Dog written and illustrated by Nina Laden

Red Fox Running by Eve Bunting, paintings by Wendell Minor

ACTIVITIES

Game
Kino learned a lesson in smells when he got sprayed by a skunk. Use this opportunity to teach about smell by creating a smelling game. Select some strong-smelling items, like ammonia, a lemon, perfume, or an onion. Liquids can be soaked into a cotton ball or a piece of paper towel. Make holes in the tops of the boxes, and cover them with thin fabric or coffee filters. Have one child at a time write a consecutive number on each box. Then have players try to identify the individual scents.

Crafts
In *The Leopard's Drum*, Osebo made a drum that everyone wanted. Make your own decorative drums out of old yogurt cups. Use a deflated balloon and a rubber band to make the top of the drum. Decorate the drums with stickers, glued-on glitter, pieces of fabric, or paper.

Outside
Look outside for pairs of young and old people or things. For example, a big old tree and a young sapling, a little bud and a full-blooming flower, a mother and her child, a big boulder and a small pebble. Afterward, discuss how these things are related and what properties are shared by the young objects and the old ones.

SHOW NUMBER 310

Guest Readers

Hector Elizondo

Joanie Bartels

Summary

Kino and Natasha are gathered with Patrick and some students in a classroom where they are talking about Thanksgiving and being thankful. Patrick reads a story about children who eat jelly and toast for Thanksgiving dinner to save the lives of the turkeys and asks the children what they could share for Thanksgiving. Natasha and Kino come up with a plan to share books with sick children at the hospital. Back at the Storyplace, they are collecting books when Hector offers to read another Thanksgiving book, about a family who wants to come to America. Afterward, Kino and Natasha make a trip to the hospital to deliver the books to the children. Joanie comes along to sing "Over the River and Through the Woods," while Natasha turns the pages.

BOOKS READ

'Twas the Night Before Thanksgiving written and illustrated by Dav Pilkey: A variation of the classic Christmas poem describes the trip of eight school children and their teacher to visit a turkey farm on the day before Thanksgiving. The children fall in love with the friendly turkeys and are horrified to learn that the farmer will kill them that night for Thanksgiving dinners. While the adults are out of eyesight, the children sneak the turkeys under their clothes, onto the bus, and back to their homes, where they all feast on veggies, jelly, and toast. This year everyone gives thanks for love and for living, especially the turkeys. (themes: holidays [Thanksgiving], friendship, sharing, caring/concern for others)

How Many Days to America? by Eve Bunting, illustrated by Beth Peck: On a West Indian island, life is nice until the day in October when soldiers come to the house. Father announces it is time to leave the country with nothing but their money. The family climbs aboard a boat that will take them to America, but along the way a part breaks and the boat cannot move. After many problems, the refugees head out to sea again. Then a boat approaches and pulls them to shore. When they reach land, the people there welcome them to America and take the passengers to sheds where they serve them food. The Americans explain that it is Thanksgiving Day, a celebration of the first immigrants. (themes: holidays [Thanksgiving], determination, feelings [fear, hope], resourcefulness, adventure, cooperation)

Over the River and Through the Woods by Lydia Maria Child, illustrated by Nadine Bernard Westcott: In a series of illustrations to the classic song, a family rushes through the snow to their grandparents' house for a Thanksgiving celebration. Meanwhile, the grandparents make the preparations for the big feast at their home. (themes: holidays [Thanksgiving], family, sharing, rhyme)

STORYPICKS

Thanksgiving at the Tappletons' by Eileen Spinelli, illustrated by Maryann Cocca-Leffler

Kashtanka by Anton Chekhov, illustrated by Gennady Spirin

ACTIVITIES

Game
Almost everybody has cranberry sauce at Thanksgiving. Fill a glass jar with cranberries and play a guessing game. Ask players to estimate how many cranberries are in the jar. When everyone has guessed, collaborate on a way to sort and count the berries, in fives, in tens, in separate groups, or in pairs.

Crafts
Make your own turkeys. Have people outline their hands on pieces of colored paper and then cut out the shape. Glue crumpled bits of colored tissue paper onto the fingers for feathers. Write a message in the body of the turkey, and offer it to a friend or a family member.

Outside
Organize a canned food drive or participate in one through a local store. Have people bring in canned foods from home that can then be donated to needy families or organizations.

Storytime™

Section C
Booklists and Resources

This section includes two booklists organized to make it easy for you to find a particular book. There is also a resource section with a glossary and a summary of research findings about literacy.

① Annotated Alphabetical Booklist

This list includes all the books read on *Storytime*, presented in alphabetical order by title and including a summary of each book and the number of the show on which it is read.

② Thematic Booklist

This list includes all of the books read on *Storytime*, organized by theme. Note that the themes are divided into general areas: Social/Emotional, Cognitive Skills, Cultural/Social Diversity, Critical Thinking/Problem-Solving, Story Types, and those particularly appropriate for 2-3-year-olds. Within each general area, books are listed alphabetically under subcategories that help you choose the books that relate most closely to a specific theme.

③ Resources

This page includes the names of several organizations that you can use as resources in different ways, as well as the names of a few good books. At the end of the guide there is a detailed bibliography that was used to gather much of the information about literacy in this guide, along with a glossary and summary of research findings.

Section C

Booklists and Resources

Annotated Alphabetical Booklist

Abuela by Arthur Dorros
Illustrated by Elisa Kleven
Rosalba and her grandmother love to explore New York City together. One day they fly up into the sky like birds and explore the city from above. They pass over the busy city, travel to Abuela's native island, rest high up in the clouds, pass the windows of Papa's work, and land back in the park for a boat ride on the lake. (themes: family [grandmother], imagination, adventure) Show #118

The Adventures of Taxi Dog
by Debra and Sal Barracca
Pictures by Mark Buehner
Maxi, a stray dog wandering around New York City, is picked up by Jim, a taxi driver. Together they travel the streets of New York picking up new people and taking them to new places across town. Maxi is happy to have finally found someone to take care of him. (themes: friendship, adventure, rhyme) Show #133

Alistair's Elephant
by Marilyn Sadler
Illustrated by Roger Bollen
The meticulous and organized Alistair is quite disturbed when he is followed home by an elephant after a trip to the zoo. He learns to adjust to the elephant and returns him the following Saturday, only to find on his way home that he is being followed by a giraffe. (themes: fantasy, problem-solving) Show #104

All Pigs Are Beautiful
by Dick King-Smith
Illustrated by Anita Jeram
A little girl who loves pigs talks about all the pigs she likes, what they do, and who they look like. Although she loves all pigs, her favorites are a black-and-white medium-snouted breed from Gloucester, and Monte, a gentle bull who loves to be scratched on top of his head and lives in the woods. (themes: animals, nature) Show #131

Amazing Grace by Mary Hoffman
Pictures by Caroline Binch
Grace loves to act out stories so she is thrilled when she hears of plans to put on Peter Pan as the class play. The other kids tell her she can't play Peter Pan because Peter isn't a girl, and he isn't black. With encouragement from her Nana, Grace proves them wrong by practicing hard to be the best Peter Pan there is. (themes: uniqueness, differences, self-esteem) Show #109

Amber on the Mountain
by Tony Johnston
Paintings by Robert Duncan
Amber lives high on the mountain, in an isolated village where few people know how to read. Then a man comes to build a road, bringing his family with him. Amber befriends his daughter, Anna, and with her help, Amber learns to read. When the road is complete, it is time for Anna to leave, and Amber is determined to teach herself to write so she can answer Anna's letters. (themes: friendship, resourcefulness, determination) Show #219

Anna and the Little Green Dragon
by Klaus Baumgart
Anna is having her breakfast one morning when a little green dragon pops out of her cornflakes box. He makes a big mess out of all the food on the table and sprays cocoa in her face, and Anna gets blamed by her mother. Her mother doesn't believe it could have been a dragon until a large dragon appears at the door looking for her son. (theme: fantasy) Show #101

Annie Bananie by Leah Komaiko
Illustrated by Laura Cornell
In rhyme, this story is about two friends who have done many adventurous things together. Then Annie Bananie has to move away, and her friend assures her that while she may find some new friends in her new home, Annie will never ever find a friend as good as her. (themes: friendship, rhyme) Show #135

Any Kind of Dog by Lynn Reiser
Richard really wants a dog, any kind of dog, but his mother says a dog would be too much trouble. She gives him a series of other kinds of animals that look like dogs, but none of them are really dogs. Finally, she gives in and gives him a real dog. It is trouble, but Richard thinks it's worth it. (themes: responsibility, animals) Show #102

The Art Lesson
by Tomie dePaola
Tomie loves art, so he can't wait to have a real art class in first grade. But when the day arrives, the teacher won't let him use his sixty-four crayons, and the assignment is to copy, something he has learned never to do. His teacher agrees to let him color his way if he completes the assignment first. (themes: uniqueness, determination) Show #132

Aunt Isabel Tells a Good One
by Kate Duke
Penelope the mouse asks her aunt to tell her a story, and together they make up a story about the adventures of Lady Nell who falls in love with Prince Augustus and rescues him from a cave so they can live happily ever after. (themes: adventure, feelings) Show #126

Babushka Baba Yaga
by Patricia Polacco
Baba Yaga is a lonely forest creature who longs to have a family of her own to care for. When she disguises herself to join the local village and takes on the care of a little boy, everyone learns an important lesson about tolerating differences. (themes: family [grandmother], feelings [loneliness], friendship, caring/concern for others, differences, fairy tale) Show #306

Babushka's Doll by Patricia Polacco
When Natasha becomes impatient on a visit to her Babushka, she is left to play with a magic temperamental doll who orders her around. Natasha is so frustrated, she learns to behave better. (themes: fantasy, responsibility) Show #120

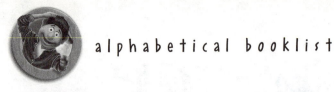

alphabetical booklist

The Baby Blue Cat Who Said No
by Ainslie Pryor
A mother cat takes very good care of her four baby cats. All of her babies like the dinner she has made and the story she has read, except the Baby Blue Cat, who always says no. (themes: family [mother], uniqueness, interactive) Show #133

Baby Rattlesnake
by Te Ata and Lynn Moroney
Illustrated by Veg Reisberg
A baby rattlesnake is eager to have his own rattle, but his parents tell him he is too young. When he convinces them to give him the rattle, he misuses it, and it is destroyed. (themes: family, responsibility, feelings [comfort]) Show #121

The Banza by Diane Wolkstein
Illustrated by Marc Brown
A tiger gives his best friend the goat a banjo to protect herself in the jungles of Haiti. When she is surrounded by tigers one day, she plays the banjo over her heart and is able to scare them away. (themes: friendship, feelings [courage], fairy tale) Show #129

Bear by John Shoenherr
A little bear wakes up to find his mother gone and finds that he must learn how to survive in the wild on his own. (themes: self-esteem, resourcefulness, animals, nature) Show #218

The Big Big Sea by Martin Waddell
Illustrated by Jennifer Eachus
A little girl and her mother enjoy a special time together at the sea. They walk to the beach at night, walk in up to their ankles, splash in the water, and make footprints. Afterward her mother carries the little girl home for hot toast by the fire. (themes: family [mother], nature)** Show #209

A Big Fat Enormous Lie
by Marjorie Weinman Sharmat
Illustrated by David McPhail
A little boy is very sorry that he told a lie — he said he didn't eat all the cookies. Now the lie is getting bigger and uglier, and it won't go away. Finally, the boy gives up and tells his parents the truth. The lie starts to get smaller and smaller until it finally disappears. (themes: family, imagination, responsibility) Show #138

The Big Pumpkin
by Erica Silverman
Illustrated by S.D. Schindler
A witch plants a pumpkin seed to make a pumpkin pie and reluctantly allows a series of ghoulish monsters to help her pull the grown pumpkin out of the ground, learning about the pleasures of sharing and friendship. (themes: holidays [Halloween], fantasy, sharing, cooperation, friendship, problem-solving) Show #301

Boodil, My Dog
by Pija Lindenbaum
A little girl describes the many ways that she loves her dog Boodil, whom no one else seems to appreciate in quite the same way. (themes: friendship, uniqueness, animals) Show #213

Borreguita and the Coyote
translated and retold by
Verna Aardema
Illustrated by Petra Mathers
Borreguita, a little lamb living at the foot of a mountain, has been targeted by a hungry wolf who wants to eat her for dinner. Through a series of resourceful tricks, she manages to protect herself and send him running far away. (themes: fairy tale, resourcefulness) Show #117

The Boy and the Ghost
by Robert D. San Souci
Illustrated by J. Brian Pinkney
A young boy from a poor family sets out to earn money for his family and encounters a wealth of riches through a ghost and a haunted house. (themes: family, fantasy, responsibility, feelings [courage]) Show #139

The Boy with Square Eyes
by Juliet and Charles Snape
Charlie watches so much television that one day his eyes become square, and everything he looks at appears to be square. At the suggestion of his doctor, he learns to look at other things, and his eyes are returned to normal. (themes: uniqueness [perspective], problem-solving) Show #114

Broderick by Edward Ormondroyd
Illustrated by John Larrecq
Broderick is a mouse who loves to eat books, until the day he comes upon a story about mice. He is inspired to do something different, despite the laughter of his peers, and becomes a world-famous surfing mouse, returning to a comfortable retirement. (themes: determination, identity) Show #134

Buz written and illustrated by
Richard Egielski
A bug named Buz finds himself swallowed by a young boy in a spoonful of cereal and chased throughout the boy's body by some pills. He manages to escape in the water at bath time, only to learn from his doctor that he has caught a bug himself. (themes: adventure, fantasy) Show #308

Cabbage Rose by M.C. Helldorfer
Illustrated by Julie Downing
Cabbage Rose is a plain girl with a talent for painting things that come to life. Through this special gift, she manages to escape her evil brothers and meet a prince, who falls in love and wants to marry her as she is. (themes: family [siblings], uniqueness, fairy tale) Show #207

The Cat Who Lost His Purr
by Michelle Coxon
A cat sets out one morning to look for his missing purr in the noises across the house. He finds that the purr comes back when the children of the house have returned. (themes: sounds, family, animals) Show #137

Chicka Chicka Boom Boom by
Bill Martin, Jr. and
John Archambault
Illustrated by Lois Ehlert
A colorful collage of letters climb up to the top of the coconut tree in a singsong rhyme. Once they get to the top, the tree sags over, and they all fall down. One by one, they dust themselves off and pick themselves up. (themes: alphabet, sounds) Show #102

Chicken Sunday
by Patricia Polacco
Natasha spends every Sunday with her neighbors, Stuart and Ninnie, and their grandma, Miss Eula. With the help of a local shopkeeper, the children manage to sell their painted eggs to earn enough money to buy Miss Eula the hat she dreams of. (themes: family, caring/concern for others, differences, friendship, resourcefulness) Show #102

alphabetical booklist

Chrysanthemum by Kevin Henkes
A little mouse named Chrysanthemum thinks her name is perfect until the day she goes to school and is teased by the other children. But when the fabulous new pregnant music teacher admires her name, Chrysanthemum learns to like it again. (themes: feelings [teasing, embarrassment], self-esteem) Show #136

Clean Your Room, Harvey Moon
by Pat Cummings
It is Saturday morning, and Harvey Moon has to clean his room before watching his favorite cartoons. He rushes through his chores, pushing the mess under the rug until his mother suggests they start working on the lumps. (themes: responsibility, rhyme) Show #133

Company's Coming
by Arthur Yorinks
Illustrated by David Small
When a spaceship lands in Shirley and Moe's yard, Moe is suspicious and calls in the army and the FBI, who quickly surround the house. But Shirley opens the present the alien visitors have brought to find that it is just what she needs—a blender. Now everyone relaxes and enjoys dinner together. (themes: sharing, differences) Show #130

Contrary Mary written and
illustrated by Anita Jeram
Mary the mouse decides one morning to do the opposite of what she is supposed to do, but when her mother does the same, Mary has a change of heart. (themes: cooperation, family [mother], feelings [love], opposites)** Show #305

Courtney written and illustrated by
John Burningham
Although the children ignore their parents' advice to get a dog with a good pedigree, the dog they bring homes turns out to be one with extraordinary talents. (themes: friendship, caring/concern for others, animals, differences) Show #304

Cuddly Dudley by Jez Alborough
Dudley the penguin loves to play alone, so one day he escapes from his siblings, who love to huddle and cuddle. But when he gets lost, he finds that he is happier than ever to huddle when he finally spots his family over the hill. (themes: family, adventure) Show #110

Daley B by Jon Blake
Illustrated by Axel Scheffler
Daley B does not know what kind of animal he is until the day that Jazzy D the weasel comes to eat a rabbit. Just in time, he uses his big feet to jump away and learns his true identity. (themes: identity, problem-solving) Show #116

Dear Mr. Blueberry by Simon James
A little girl who loves whales carries on a correspondence with Mr. Blueberry about the whale she seems to have in her pond. Mr. Blueberry is quite doubtful about her whale, but the little girl cheerfully continues until the day it is time to say good-bye to her whale. (themes: fantasy, nature) Show #133

Dinner at the Panda Palace
by Stephanie Calmenson
Illustrated by Nadine B. Westcott
In this counting book, groups of animals come in to dine at the restaurant owned by Mr. Panda. (themes: rhyme, counting, animals)** Show 136

Dogteam by Gary Paulsen
A team of dogs pulls a sled through a cold and snowy night, admiring and observing the winter forest landscape. (themes: animals, feelings [happiness], nature) Show #206

Do Not Open by Brinton Turkle
Miss Moody finds a purple bottle on the beach after a storm. Despite a warning on the outside, she opens it up, releasing a monster of smoke. She tricks the creature into turning himself into a mouse, who is promptly eaten by her cat. (themes: fantasy, feelings [courage, curiosity]) Show #131

¿Donde Esta Mi Osito?
by Jez Alborough
When Eduardito loses his teddy bear, he heads into the forest to find it. There he finds a big bear who has lost his teddy bear too. They quickly change bears, and Eduardito runs for the safety of home. (themes: cooperation, problem-solving, feelings [fear]) Show #211

Donna O'Neeshuck Was Chased by Some Cows by Bill Grossman
Illustrated by Sue Truesdell
Donna O'Neeshuck gives a cow a pat on the head and finds herself being chased by the cow and her friends. Along the way, others join in the chase, all enjoying Donna's pats on the head. (themes: adventure, rhyme, sequence of events) Show #216

Don't Fidget a Feather
by Erica Silverman
Illustrated by S.D. Schindler
Duck and Gander can't seem to stop competing with each other. Their "freeze-in-place contest" continues until Fox is about to put Gander in a stew. Finally Duck moves to save his friend, and both are declared winners. (theme: friendship) Show #216

The Doorbell Rang by Pat Hutchins
A mother has baked a batch of cookies for her children at teatime, but as the doorbell keeps ringing, new friends arrive and the cookies must be divided and shared. At last Grandma arrives with more cookies for everyone. (themes: friendship, sharing, counting, interactive)** Show #134

The Dragon of an Ordinary Family
by Margaret Mahy
Illustrated by Helen Oxenbury
The Belsackis are a very ordinary family until the day that Mr. Belsacki brings home a dragon as a pet. When the dragon grows too big to keep, the family escorts him to a magic land in a very extraordinary vacation. (themes: fantasy, family) Show #117

Duckat by Gaelyn Gordon
Illustrated by Chris Gaskin
When a duck arrives at Mabel's doorstep acting like a cat, she does everything she can to set him straight. Just as she succeeds in convincing him he is a duck, a cat arrives who acts like a duck. (themes: imagination, differences, animals, identity) Show #123

Earl's Too Cool for Me
by Leah Komaiko
Illustrated by Laura Cornell
In rhyme, a girl describes a boy named Earl, a cool kid who has done a series of amazing things. (themes: rhyme, friendship, interactive) Show #135

Eddie and Teddy by Gus Clarke
Eddie and his bear, Teddy, are always together until it is time for Eddie to go to school for the first time. Gradually Eddie learns to like school, but Teddy is so lonely that the teacher agrees to let him come too. (themes: friendship, feelings [sadness]) Show #119

Effie by Beverley Allinson
Illustrated by Barbara Reid
Effie the ant has a very loud voice, which causes all of the other ants and insects to flee. Then one day Effie saves everyone from a giant foot, by telling it, in her loud voice, to stop. (themes: nature, problem-solving, differences) Show #128

alphabetical booklist

Elmer by David McKee
Elmer is a patchwork-colored elephant who makes everyone laugh and keeps them happy. But he doesn't like being different, so he paints himself gray. The other elephants liked him better the other way, so when the rain washes his paint, they celebrate Elmer Day by painting each other in colors. (themes: friendship, differences, colors, uniqueness) Show #118

Elvira by Margaret Shannon
Elvira is tormented by other dragons for not eating princesses or rolling in the mud. When she wanders far away and becomes like a princess herself, she is almost eaten by her parents. They take her home, and all of the other dragons now want to be like Elvira. (themes: differences, uniqueness, identity) Show #221

The Emperor's New Clothes retold and illustrated by S.T. Mendelson
In this version of the classic tale about a vain emperor, the characters are animals. (themes: identity, feelings [vanity], fairy tale) Show #123

The Empty Pot by Demi
The emperor, who loves flowers, gives all the children one seed and says that the child with the best flower at the end of the year will succeed him. Only Ping, who also loves flowers, has the courage to admit that he could not make the seed grow, and he is named the successor. (themes: responsibility, nature) Show #202

Engelbert the Elephant
by Tom Paxton
Illustrated by Steven Kellogg
Engelbert receives an invitation to the queen's ball, but, when he arrives, the other guests run from him in fear. The queen invites Engelbert to dance, and he is the hit of the party. (themes: adventure, rhyme, differences) Show #130

Fairy Went A-Marketing
by Rose Fyleman
Illustrated by Jamichael Henterly
A young fairy makes a series of trips to the market, where she buys a fish in a bowl, a bird in a cage, and a mouse in a basket, all of whom she sets free. (theme: feelings [generosity]) Show # 217

Farmer Duck by Martin Waddell
Illustrated by Helen Oxenbury
A duck is forced to do all the work while the lazy farmer lounges in bed. The other animals decide to help their friend by chasing away the farmer and helping to share the responsibility of the farm. (theme: cooperation) Show #127

First Pink Light
by Eloise Greenfield
Illustrated by Jan Spivey Gilchrist
A young boy is eager to stay up all night and wait for his father, who has been away for a long time. He convinces his mother to let him wait in the rocking chair but falls asleep before dawn, when his father returns to put him to bed. (themes: family [father], feelings [excitement]) Show #137

The Fish Who Could Wish
by John Bush
Illustrated by Korky Paul
A fish with the ability to wish for anything he wants one day wishes he could be like all the other fish, thus losing his unique gift. (themes: self-esteem, uniqueness) Show #113

Five Bad Boys, Billy Que and the Dustdobbin by Susan Patron
Illustrated by Mike Shenon
When Billy Que is shrunk down to size by the angry Dustdobbin under his bed, five bad boys come along to help him out. The Dustdobbin agrees to return Billy to his former size, and the two promise to keep out of each other's way. (themes: fantasy, feelings [anger], size) Show #103

A Flea in the Ear
by Stephen Wyllie
Illustrated by Ken Brown
A flea-ridden dog is so desperate to get rid of his itchy fleas that he almost loses the hens he is guarding to the wily fox. (themes: animals, responsibility, problem-solving) Show # 308

Flower Garden by Eve Bunting
Illustrated by Kathryn Hewitt
A little girl and her father prepare a window box of beautiful flowers for her mother's birthday. (themes: family, sharing, nature) Show #212

The Folks in the Valley
by Jim Aylesworth
Illustrated by Stefano Vitale
This colorful alphabet book is filled with objects and activities from Amish life. (themes: alphabet, differences) Show #129

The Fortune-Tellers
by Lloyd Alexander
Illustrated by Trina Schart Hyman
An unhappy carpenter visits a fortune-teller who promises that he will be rich and happy. In a case of mistaken identity, the carpenter takes on the fortune-teller's trade and fulfills his prophecy. (theme: fairy tale) Show #127

Franklin in the Dark
by Paulette Bourgeois
Illustrated by Brenda Clark
A young turtle who is afraid of small, dark places meets a series of animals who have all conquered their fears. He learns to conquer his fear by using a night light before he goes to sleep in his shell. (themes: feelings [fear], differences, problem-solving, resourcefulness) Show #114

Frog Went A-Courtin'
retold by John Langstaff
Pictures by Feodor Rojankovsky
This illustrated version of an old song tells the story of a frog who courts Miss Mouse, gets Uncle Rat's consent, plans a wedding feast, invites the other animals as guests, and enjoys a honeymoon in Paris, France. (themes: rhyme, music) Show #214

Froggy Gets Dressed
by Jonathan London
Illustrated by Frank Remkiewicz
When Froggy wakes up to find snow outside, he is so eager to get out and play that he starts outside without getting completely dressed. With the help of reminders from his mother, he must dress and undress as he remembers each article needed. (themes: family [mother], responsibility) Show #116

La Gallinita Roja
by Margot Zemach
This is a Spanish-language version of the classic story about a little red hen who works hard to plant a seed of wheat, help it grow, harvest the crop, and bake a cake with the flour without the help of her lazy animal friends. (themes: cooperation, responsibility) Show #211

The Ghost-Eye Tree
by Bill Martin, Jr. and John Archambault
Illustrated by Ted Rand
A boy and his sister are sent to get more milk but must pass the scary ghost-eye tree on the way there. Together they race past the tree, and though she teases him for being afraid, the brother bravely rushes back for his hat when he loses it along the way. (themes: family [siblings], feelings [fear, courage], adventure) Show #121

alphabetical booklist

Ghost's Hour, Spook's Hour
by Eve Bunting
Illustrated by Donald Carrick
A little boy and his dog wake up in the middle of the night and explore the scary noises all over the house. After finding the causes of each noise, they curl up with the boy's parents, whom they find sleeping in the living room. (themes: feelings [fear, courage], sounds) Show #116

The Gingerbread Man
by Eric A. Kimmel
Illustrated by Megan Lloyd
An old couple make a gingerbread man who hops to the floor and runs out the door. This starts a chase that attracts a whole series of animals and ends as the gingerbread man is eaten by a hungry fox. (themes: fairy tale, resourcefulness) Show #106

Go Away, Big Green Monster!
by Ed Emberley
This is a color cut-out book of different colors and shapes that accumulate to create a big green monster and then slowly come apart to make him disappear. (themes: feelings [fear], shapes/colors)** Show #115

Going Home by Margaret Wild
Illustrated by Wayne Harris
As Hugo recovers in the hospital next door to a zoo, he is carried each night on a magical trip with one of the animals, who takes to him to a special faraway place. At last it is time to go home, and Hugo encourages his roommates to take the trips when he is gone. (themes: imagination, feelings [homesickness], friendship, adventure) Show #204

Goldilocks and the Three Bears
retold and illustrated by Jan Brett
In this colorfully illustrated version of the classic tale, a little girl comes upon the home of three bears, eats the small bear's porridge, breaks his chair, sleeps in his bed, and is chased home upon their return. (themes: fairy tale, responsibility, size) Show #137

Gorilla by Anthony Browne
A lonely girl who loves gorillas is given a toy gorilla on her birthday. At night the gorilla comes to life, and together they visit the zoo until it is time to return home, where the gorilla becomes a toy again. (themes: family [father], feelings [loneliness], fantasy) Show #132

Grandpa's Face
by Eloise Greenfield
Illustrated by Floyd Cooper
Tamika loves her grandfather, who is an actor; but one day, while he is rehearsing, she sees a scary, mean face she does not know. When he learns of her fear, he assures her that he was only practicing and that she will never see that face directed at her. (themes: family [grandfather], feelings [fear, love]) Show #120

The Grasshopper and the Ants
retold by Margaret Wise Brown
Illustrated by Larry Moore
A playful grasshopper sings and dances all summer long while the ants are working hard storing up for the long winter. When he is overcome by cold and hunger, the ants take him in in exchange for his musical entertainment, and he learns to sing a more grateful song. (themes: sharing, responsibility, music) Show #203

Green Wilma by Tedd Arnold
One day Wilma wakes up green, lets out a croak, and chases a buzzing fly. She seems to have turned into a frog. She causes a commotion at school, hops out the door to follow a fly, and wakes up to find that she was dreaming on her log. (themes: fantasy, identity) Show #113

Greetings from Sandy Beach
by Bob Graham
A family piles into their car for a vacation at the beach. With the help of a group of dangerous-looking bikers and an unruly crowd of school kids, they set up their tent, play in the water, and manage to have a good time. (themes: family, adventure, cooperation) Show #125

The Grumpalump by Sarah Hayes
Illustrated by Barbara Firth
One by one animals approach a big "grumpalump," or a lump that grumps, to determine what it is. No one can tell until the gun blew, and the lump turns into a hot airship that flies off into the sky. (themes: rhyme, problem-solving) Show #204

The Gullywasher written and illustrated by Joyce Rossi
While waiting for a storm to pass, a young girl hears a tall tale from her grandfather about how he changed from being a young cowboy to the older man he is today. (themes: family [grandfather], fantasy, imagination, nature) Show #304

Halloween Howls: Riddles That Are a Scream written and illustrated by Giulio Maestro
A series of riddles revolving around the theme of Halloween. (themes: holidays [Halloween], rhymes [riddles]) Show #301

The Happy Day by Ruth Krauss
Illustrated by Marc Simont
Snow is falling while the animals are sleeping. Gradually the animals wake up, sniff around them, and run together to a place in the snow where they find a single yellow flower, the only sign of color in a black-and-white winter. (themes: animals, nature, colors)** Show #110

The Happy Hedgehog Band
by Martin Waddell
Illustrated by Jill Barton
Harry the hedgehog makes a drum, and the other hedgehogs are so impressed that they make their own drums to form a band. When the other animals admire their music, Harry encourages them to join in by contributing their own special noises to the band. (themes: friendship, music, resourcefulness) Show #124

A Hat for Minerva Louise
by Janet Morgan Stoeke
Minerva Louise the hen wants to explore the snow, but it is too cold. She searches the farmyard for something to use as a hat until she finds just the right thing — a pair of mittens she can use to cover her head and her tail. (themes: adventure, problem-solving, resourcefulness)** Show #206

Hi! by Ann Herbert Scott
Illustrated by Glo Coalson
While waiting in line with her mother at the post office, Margarita greets every entering customer with a cheerful "Hi!" When no one responds, her "Hi" gets quieter until she is greeted cheerfully herself by the clerk behind the window. (themes: interactive, friendship) Show #219**

Honey Paw and Lightfoot
by Jonathan London
Illustrated by Jon Van Zyle
A mother teaches her bear cub how to survive in the wild, hunt for food, and defend himself against predators so that he can go off someday on his own. (themes: animals, family [mother], resourcefulness, nature) Show #309

alphabetical booklist

Horton Hatches the Egg
by Dr. Seuss
Faithful Horton agrees to sit on an egg for Maisey, the lazy bird. He weathers out the seasons, tolerates the teasing of his friends, and puts up with his sale to the circus to protect the egg — because he promised Maisey that's what he would do. (themes: animals, responsibility, caring/concern for others) Show #111

A House Is a House for Me
by Mary Ann Hoberman
Illustrated by Betty Fraser
This picture book describes in rhyme all the many kinds of houses for all the animals, vehicles, people, and things all over the earth. (themes: rhyme, vocabulary, nature) Show #210

The House That Drac Built
by Judy Sierra
Illustrated by Will Hillenbrand
In a retelling of the classic cumulative rhyme, a series of Halloween monsters create havoc until a group of trick-or-treaters arrive to set things straight. (themes: holidays [Halloween], fantasy, feelings [fear], sequence of events) Show #301

How Many Days to America?
by Eve Bunting
Illustrated by Beth Peck
A group of refugees travel to America on a boat, facing hunger and adversity, and are welcomed to American soil by people celebrating Thanksgiving. (themes: holidays [Thanksgiving], determination, feelings [hope], resourcefulness, adventure, cooperation) Show #310

The Hungry Thing
by Jan Slepian and Ann Seidler
Pictures by Richard E. Martin
A very hungry thing arrives in town one day, requesting food in very funny ways. When a little boy is able to decipher what the thing says, it can be fed until it is full. (themes: rhyme, caring/concern for others, problem-solving) Show #118

The Hunter by Paul Geraghty
While collecting honey with her grandfather, Jemima plays at being hunted, wanders too far, and gets lost. When she finds a baby elephant whose mother has been killed by real hunters, she helps to lead it back to its herd and resolves never to be a hunter again. (themes: family, adventure, caring/concern for others, nature) Show #218

Hunting the White Cow
by Tres Seymour
Pictures by Wendy Anderson Halperin
When the white cow runs away from the barn to hide in the tobacco patch, no one can bring her back. The men set out in increasingly larger groups, but no one can convince the cow to come back home, not even the little girl who is determined to try herself. (themes: problem-solving, cooperation) Show #215

I Hear a Noise by Diane Goode
A little boy hears a noise, and though his mother tells him it is nothing, a big dragon swoops down to carry him off with the monster in the sky. When the mother dragon learns what her child has done, she orders him to take the boy home where he belongs. (themes: family [mother], fantasy, feelings [fear]) Show #127

If written and illustrated by Sarah Perry
A colorful series of illustrations depicts all sorts of fantastic scenarios and encourages the reader to think up some more. (themes: imagination, fantasy) Show #308

If You Give a Mouse a Cookie
by Laura Joffe Numeroff
Illustrated by Felicia Bond
A mouse arrives at a boy's house and asks him for a cookie. When this request is granted, a new one is made, and the boy is led all over the house through a series of chores for his visitor. (theme: sequence of events) Show #112

I'm Coming to Get You! written and illustrated by Tony Ross
A frightening monster hurls through outer space, coming to get little Tommy Brown, only to find that he is smaller than the boy's shoe. (themes: feelings [fear, relief], fantasy, size) Show #307

Ira Sleeps Over by Bernard Waber
Ira is afraid to sleep over at his friend Reggie's house without his teddy bear, but he doesn't want Reggie to think he is a baby, either. When he learns that Reggie has a bear of his own to sleep with, he rushes home for his teddy and everyone can sleep together. (themes: feelings [fear], friendship) Show #104

Is Your Mama a Llama?
by Deborah Guarino
Illustrated by Steven Kellogg
A young llama asks a series of animal friends about their mothers and learns the distinguishing characteristics of each one, including his own, who is a llama. (themes: rhyme, animals, identity, family [mother], interactive) Show #302

It's the Bear! by Jez Alborough
Eddie is nervous about having a picnic with his mother in the woods, where he knows there is a big bear. While his mother goes back for the pie they forgot, the bear arrives and eats up their lunch, turning to Eddie for dessert. His mother returns with the pie, the two flee, and the bear can have his dessert. (themes: feelings [fear], rhyme)** Show #218

The Itsy Bitsy Spider
by Iza Trapani
This illustrated version of the popular song with hand motions adds a few extra verses. After a series of unsuccessful climbs, the spider finally makes it to the top of the maple tree, spins a web, and takes a nice rest in the sun. (themes: nature, music)** Show #131

Jamberry by Bruce Degen
A boy and a bear recite in rhyme about different berries and how much they love them. (theme: rhyme) Show #121

Jessica written and illustrated by Kevin Henkes
Ruthie Simms has an imaginary friend, and they do everything together. Then it is time to start school, and Ruthie finds a new friend, who is even better. (themes: friendship, imagination, family) Show #307

Jonathan and His Mommy
by Irene Smalls-Hector
Illustrated by Michael Hays
Jonathan loves to take walks with his Mommy. Together they take big steps, little steps, side steps, and scissors steps all across the neighborhood. (themes: family [mother], identity)** Show #107

Julius, the Baby of the World
by Kevin Henkes
Lily has a new baby brother whom her parents adore and who she thinks is disgusting. She taunts him in his crib and wishes he would go away, until the day a cousin calls Julius disgusting. Lily defends her baby brother, admiring and kissing him and making her cousin do the same. (themes: family [siblings], feelings [jealousy, love]) Show #124

alphabetical booklist

King Bidgood's in the Bathtub
by Audrey Wood
Illustrated by Don Wood
The page enlists the help of various members of the kingdom to help get the king out of the bathtub. Nothing that any of them can do convinces the king to get out until the page decides to pull the plug in the bathtub. (themes: interactive, problem-solving, sequence of events) Show #205

Knock, Knock, Teremok!
adapted and illustrated by
Katya Arnold
A series of progressively larger animals knock at the door of an empty hut and move in to stay. When a big bear arrives and finds there is no room, he climbs to the roof, and the whole thing caves in. (themes: sharing, problem-solving, sequence of events) Show #203

Lady Bugatti by Joyce Maxner
Illustrated by Kevin Hawkes
In a vividly illustrated book, a ladybug hosts a very formal dinner party for a few of her closest insect friends. Afterward, she takes them to a show, at the end of which she gives the prize for the best performance to the owl. (themes: friendship, animals, vocabulary) Show #112

The Last Time I Saw Harris
by Frank Remkiewicz
Edmond is teaching the colors to Harris, his parrot, but Harris is carried away in a windstorm before he can learn purple. Edmond sets out with the chauffeur and his flash cards across the world to find Harris, who finds them by identifying the purple hood of their car. (themes: friendship, adventure, colors) Show #119

The Leopard's Drum retold by
Jessica Souhami
Osebo the Leopard has a magnificent drum that he won't share with anyone else, so Nyame the Sky God offers a reward to the animal who will bring him the drum. (themes: fairy tale, animals, sharing, resourcefulness, problem-solving) Show #309

Life Is Fun by Nancy Carlson
This book is a list of instructions for living on earth and being happy. Be nice, eat healthy food once in a while, get exercise, feel free to cry when you are sad, laugh a lot, fall in love, and you will be awesome. (theme: feelings [happiness]) Show #139

Listen, Buddy by Helen Lester
Illustrated by Lynn Munsinger
Buddy the rabbit has two beautiful ears, but he doesn't know how to listen, until a run-in with the Scruffy Varmint shows him that he had better learn to pay attention to what people tell him. (themes: cooperation, responsibility) Show #307

Little Lumpty by Miko Imai
Ignoring the fate of the famous Humpty Dumpty and the warnings of his mother, Little Lumpty sets out to see the top of the big wall. When he gets stuck at the top, the whole town joins together to help him back down. (themes: fairy tale, feelings [fear], adventure) Show #203

The Little Mouse, the Red Ripe Strawberry and the Big Hungry Bear by Don and Audrey Wood
Illustrated by Don Wood
A little mouse finds a delicious ripe strawberry but is encouraged by the narrator to share it. (themes: sharing, feelings [fear]) Show #309

The Little Old Lady Who Was Not Afraid of Anything
by Linda Williams
Illustrated by Megan Lloyd
A brave old lady is haunted by the different parts of a scary body and resolves the problem by putting them together as a scarecrow in her garden. (themes: holidays [Halloween], fantasy, feelings [courage, fear], resourcefulness, problem-solving) Show #301

Little Peep by Jack Kent
An arrogant cock controls the farmyard and intimidates the other animals, who all believe that the sun comes up because the rooster crows. When Little Peep, a new chick, tries out a crow of his own, the farmer turns on the lights, the animals think the sun has risen, and the whole farm is thrown into confusion. (themes: self-esteem, animals, cause and effect) Show #112

Little Polar Bear by Hans de Beer
While on his first hunting trip with his father, Lars the polar bear is lost at sea on a piece of ice. He is carried to a tropical land, where he meets Henry the hippo. With the help of Marcus the eagle and Samson the whale, he is carried back home to his father. (themes: animals, adventure) Show #101

The Little Red Hen
by Paul Galdone
A cat, a dog, a mouse, and a hen all live together in a house. After the animals refuse to help the hen tend her wheat, which she bakes into a delicious cake, she announces that since she did all the work by herself, she will eat the cake all by herself. From then on, all the animals are eager to help with household chores. (themes: cooperation, responsibility) Show #130

Maebelle's Suitcase
by Tricia Tusa
One-hundred-eight-year-old Maebelle, who loves birds and lives in a tree house, is putting the finishing touches on her entry for the local hat contest when Binkle flies in to borrow a suitcase for his trip south. When the suitcase becomes too heavy for Binkle to fly with, Maebelle asks for the items inside to add to her hat, saving his pride and allowing him to fly south before it gets too cold. (themes: friendship, problem-solving) Show #122

Maggie and the Pirate
by Ezra Jack Keats
Maggie has a pet cricket named Nicki that she keeps in a cage made by her father. When the cage is stolen by "the pirate" and Nicki is drowned in a tussle, Maggie learns to forgive the new boy who stole it and accepts the new cricket he has brought. (themes: friendship, feelings) Show #110

The Magic House
by Robyn H. Eversole
Illustrated by Peter Palagonia
April and her family live in a magic house full of special things, like a waterfall on the stairs, which her older sister Meredith does not see. But when Meredith is having trouble with her swan dance for ballet, April leads her to the waterfall, where Meredith begins to look more and more like a swan. (themes: family [siblings], imagination) Show #105

Magic Spring by Nami Rhee
An old man and his wife are forced to work hard and alone because they have no child, but when they sip from a magic spring, they magically become young again. Their greedy, rich neighbor rushes to do the same, only to drink too much and shrink down to being a baby. The couple arrive too late to save him but at last they have the child they have always wanted. (themes: fairy tale, feelings [greed]) Show #113

alphabetical booklist

Mama, Do You Love Me?
by Barbara M. Joosse
Illustrated by Barbara Lavallee
An Eskimo girl asks her mother questions about how much she loves her. (themes: family [mother], feelings [love]) Show #103

The Man Who Kept His Heart in a Bucket by Sonia Levitin
Illustrated by Jerry Pinkney
A man who carries his broken heart in a bucket feels nothing when he eats pie, hears music, and sees a baby. Then, a lovely maiden steals his heart and will only return it when he solves the riddle of three golden scales. He sees a scale at the baker, where this time the pie warms his heart; he identifies the musical scales that this time inspire him to dance, and recognizes the scales on the fish being carried by the father of a baby, whom he wants for his own. As he solves the riddle, he realizes his heart is in the right place and marries the beautiful maiden. (themes: feelings [love], friendship, fairy tale) Show #217

Maxi, the Hero
by Debra and Sal Barracca
Illustrated by Mark Buehner
This story, told in rhyme, follows the adventures of Maxi, who rides around New York City in a taxi with his friend Jim, the driver. When they come upon a woman whose purse has been stolen, Maxi chases the thief until the police arrive to take him away. Maxi is a hero. (themes: rhyme, caring/concern for others) Show #134

Ming Lo Moves the Mountain
by Arnold Lobel
Ming Lo goes to a wise man for help moving the large mountain whose rocks drop on his roof and whose shadow hangs over his garden. He finally solves his problem by following the advice to take apart his house, walk backward away from the mountain, and rebuild in a new spot. (themes: fairy tale, problem-solving) Show #139

Mirette on the Highwire written and illustrated by
Emily Arnold McCully
When a retired tightrope walker arrives at her mother's boardinghouse, Mirette is inspired to learn how to walk the highwire. After he teaches her his tricks, she is able to use her new talents to help him conquer the fear that sent him into retirement. (themes: detemination, caring/concern for others, friendship) Show #303

Miss Spider's Tea Party written and illustrated by David Kirk
Lonely Miss Spider sips tea in her web, wishing the other insects would join her. One by one, they turn down her invitations to tea, afraid that she will catch them in her web. But when a moth accidentally falls into the web and Miss Spider helps him and offers him tea, he tells the others of her kindness, and soon everyone joins them in the web. (themes: friendship, counting, rhyme, feelings [loneliness]) Show #221

The Mitten by Jan Brett
A little boy gets a new white mitten from his grandmother and immediately loses it against the snow. A growing crowd of increasingly large animals crawl in and stretch it out. Then, when a mouse crawls in and tickles the bear's nose, he lets out a sneeze that sends the mitten up into the air against the blue sky, and the boy is able to find it again. (themes: responsibility, animals, sequence of events) Show #135

Mole's Hill by Lois Ehlert
The mole lives in a hill that is blocking the path to the water. When fox and raccoon ask him to move his home, the mole makes the hill bigger, plants flowers, and digs a tunnel for the other animals to go through, and everyone is happy. (themes: sharing, problem-solving, animals, cooperation) Show #217

The Monkey and the Crocodile written and illustrated by
Paul Galdone
A wily monkey uses a variety of clever tricks to escape a very hungry and very greedy crocodile. (themes: feelings [greed], resourcefulness, animals) Show #302

Monster Mama by Liz Rosenberg
Illustrated by Stephen Gammell
Patrick Edward's mother is a monster, so she doesn't come out very often. When she sends him out for dessert one day, Patrick Edward is teased by a group of boys, who eat his dessert. Monster Mama hears his scream, orders the boys to make a new dessert and assures her son that she will always be there for him because she loves him. (themes: family [mother], feelings [teasing, love], sharing) Show #105

More, More, More, Said the Baby
by Vera B. Williams
This book shows different babies and the people who love them, playing with them affectionately, tossing and hugging them, looking at their toes and bellies. (themes: family, differences)** Show #120

Morris's Disappearing Bag
by Rosemary Wells
It's Christmas day, and nobody seems very interested in the bear that Morris got. But when he opens his last present, a disappearing bag, everyone suddenly wants to share and try the bag for themselves. (themes: family, sharing) Show #126

A Mother for Choco
by Keiko Kasza
A lonely little bird without a mother sets out to find one. But none of the other animals look enough like him to be his mother. Then he meets Mrs. Bear, who comforts Choco and offers to take him home to her other children — a pig, a hippo, and an alligator. (themes: family [mother], differences, feelings [comfort], animals) Show #108

Mouse's Birthday by Jane Yolen
Illustrated by Bruce Degen
It is Mouse's birthday, but his house is very small. One by one the animals squeeze their way in with their presents. Then Mouse blows out his candles, which blows the house apart. The whole barn becomes his new house, and now there is plenty of room for everyone. (themes: friendship, rhyme, size) Show #107

My Little Brother by Debi Gliori
A little girl is irritated by her pesky little brother and tries a variety of magic spells to try to get rid of him. Nothing works until the night she wakes up to find that his bed is empty and she realizes that she misses him. (themes: family [siblings], feelings [love, relief]) Show #136

My Little Red Car
by Chris L. Demarest
A little boy dreams of traveling around the world in his little red car. (themes: adventure, nature) Show #105

My Mama Had a Dancing Heart
by Libba Moore Gray
Illustrated by Raul Colon
A young girl and her mother dance their way through the four seasons of the year. (themes: family [mother], feelings [happiness], nature) Show #303

My Mom Is Excellent
by Nick Butterworth
A little boy tells about all the different ways that his mother is excellent. (theme: family [mother])** Show #109

alphabetical booklist

Nathaniel Willy, Scared Silly by Judith Mathews and Fay Robinson Illustrated by Alexi Natchev

One night, Nathaniel Willy is too frightened by the squeak in his bedroom door to fall asleep. His grandma brings in a series of different animals from the barn to help him sleep, but it is the wise woman down the road who thinks to oil the hinges of the door so Nathaniel Willy can go to sleep. (themes: family [grandmother], feelings [fear], problem-solving, animals) Show #212

Night Tree by Eve Bunting Illustrated by Ted Rand

On the night before Christmas, a boy and his family celebrate their annual ritual of decorating a special tree in a forest with goodies for the animals and gathering around it to sing Christmas carols. (themes: holidays [Christmas], family, sharing, music, nature) Show #122

Noisy Nora by Rosemary Wells

The only way that Nora seems to get noticed by her family is to make a lot of noise. When they tell her to be quiet, she decides to disappear, but they miss her so much she decides to come back. (themes: family, feelings [being left out], rhyme) Show #128

Not So Fast, Songololo by Niki Daly

Malousi lives in a big noisy family without enough money for new shoes — he wears old hand-me-down sneakers with big holes. Then one day he goes on a special trip with his grandmother, GoGo, who needs his help with her shopping in town. They head off through the noise and traffic, returning with a brand new pair of red sneakers. (themes: family [grandmother], caring/concern for others) Show #138

Nothing at All by Denys Cazet

In the farmyard, as each of the animals wakes up, the scarecrow says nothing at all until a mouse gets into his pants and he wriggles and flips across the field, breaking into several pieces. The other animals rush to put him together just in time for breakfast. (themes: interactive, animals, sounds)** Show #216

The Old Dog by Charlotte Zolotow Illustrated by James Ransome

A young boy wakes one morning to find that his old dog is dead, and the boy must find a way to go through his daily routine without him. (themes: animals, feelings [sadness], friendship) Show #306

The Old Ladies Who Liked Cats by Carol Greene Illustrated by Loretta Krupinski

The safety of an island town is threatened when the mayor issues a ban on letting cats out at night, which disrupts a sequence of events that leads to the army being nourished by the milk from the cows. Balance is restored when the ban is lifted, the sequence can continue, and the army can defend from invaders. (themes: cooperation, nature, resourcefulness, sequence of events) Show #104

Ollie Knows Everything by Abby Levine Illustrated by Lynn Munsinger

Herbert feels as though his older brother knows everything, until the day Ollie is lost on the subway on a visit to New York City. Herbert is sorry he was jealous as they search for Ollie, and when they return to their hotel to find Ollie waiting for them, he realizes that Ollie does know everything, but he is glad to have him back. (themes: family [siblings], feelings [fear, relief], problem-solving) Show #205

One of Three by Angela Johnson Illustrated by David Soman

Three sisters do everything together, but sometimes the youngest is left out. But at these times she finds she can be one of a different three, with her parents, which is just as nice. (themes: family [siblings], feelings [being left out]) Show #119

Over the River and Through the Woods by Lydia Maria Child Illustrated by Nadine Bernard Westcott

An illustrated version of the classic song alternates pictures of a family traveling through the snow to Thanksgiving dinner and the grandparents who are preparing the feast for their arrival. (themes: holidays [Thanksgiving], family, sharing, rhyme) Show #310

Owl Babies by Martin Waddell Illustrated by Patrick Benson

Three little owls are left alone one night to comfort each other while their mother is gone. Just as they start to imagine the worst, she arrives home to their nest. (themes: family [mother], feelings [sadness, comfort, fear]) Show #108

Owl Eyes by Frieda Gates Illustrated by Yoshi Miyake

As Raweno, the master of all spirits, is making all the woodland creatures, Owl continues to pester and interrupt him. Raweno retaliates by giving him the physical features he has today — a pushed-down head that he cannot turn, widened eyes so he will learn to watch, raised ears so he will learn to listen, and a brown color so no one will see him. (themes: fairy tale, animals) Show #220

The Painter written and illustrated by Peter Catalanotto

A young girl describes a day in her life with her father, who is a painter. The day culminates in a special visit to his studio. (themes: family [father], sharing) Show #306

The Paper Princess by Elisa Kleven

A little girl makes a princess out of paper, but before she can finish, the paper doll is carried away by the wind on a series of adventures until the two are happily reunited on the little girl's birthday. (themes: adventure, differences, friendship) Show #209

The Perfect Orange: A Tale from Ethiopia by Frank P. Araujo, Ph.D. Illustrated by Xiao Jun Li

A generous orphan finds a perfect orange, which she offers to her ruler, the Great Nigus, and is rewarded with wealth for her kindness. A greedy hyena tries to make a similar trade by offering all of his land but is rewarded with the perfect orange. (themes: feelings [generosity, greed], caring/concern for others, sharing, fairy tale) Show #305

Pigs Aplenty, Pigs Galore! by David McPhail

One night, a man comes downstairs to find his kitchen overrun by pigs, eating and munching away. When a pizza is delivered and the man gets the bill, he kicks the pigs out but relents when they agree to clean up. (themes: rhyme, fantasy) Show #213

Pip's Magic by Ellen Stoll Walsh

Pip is a young lizard who is afraid of the dark and sets off on a trip through a series of dark places to get help from Abra, the wizard. When he finally reaches the wise old turtle, he finds that he has conquered his fear on his own. (themes: feelings [fear, courage], determination) Show #207

alphabetical booklist

Playing Right Field by Willy Welch
Illustrated by Marc Simont
A little boy who is always picked last for baseball thinks that he is just no good. He sits out in right field daydreaming, until the day he finds everyone looking at him and a baseball lands in his glove. (themes: self-esteem, cooperation, rhyme) Show #215

A Porcupine Named Fluffy
by Helen Lester
Illustrated by Lynn Munsinger
Fluffy the porcupine is ashamed of his name until he meets a similarly misnamed rhino. (themes: friendship, identity, self-esteem, feelings [embarrassment]) Show #126

Possum Come A-Knockin'
by Nancy Van Laan
Illustrated by George Booth
The members of a large family are all busy doing their own noisy thing when a possum comes to knock on the door. One by one they stop what they are doing to see who it is, then one by one start up again when the possum hides behind a tree. (themes: family, sequence of events) Show #118

Princess Smartypants
by Babette Cole
Princess Smartypants never wants to marry, so she sets up an impossible contest for her hand that none of the princes can possibly win. When Prince Swashbuckle actually does win, she gives him a kiss that turns him into a toad. Now no one wants to marry her, and she can live happily ever after by herself. (themes: fairy tale, uniqueness) Show #140

Prize in the Snow
by Bill Easterling
Illustrated by Mary Beth Owens
A young boy, eager to be a big hunter like the older kids, sets out one morning with a box and a carrot to catch a rabbit or a bird. When he manages to trap a rabbit, he is overcome by pity for the starving and freezing animal. He sets it free and offers it some food. (themes: caring/concern for others, nature) Show #206

Pug, Slug and Doug the Thug
by Carol Saller
Illustrated by Vicki Jo Redenbaugh
When Pug, Slug and Doug the Thug come to town, there is a showdown at the saloon, and a young boy sets off a sequence of events, using the straw in his mouth, that leads to their eventual arrest. (themes: sequence of events, resourcefulness) Show #215

The Rat and the Tiger
by Keiko Kasza
Rat and Tiger are best friends, but because he is smaller, Rat always seems to get the short end of the stick. When he confronts Tiger and refuses to play, they learn to take turns and split things down the middle, until they face a new problem — the new rhino on the block. (themes: friendship, cooperation, size) Show #210

Regina's Big Mistake
by Marissa Moss
Regina is having a hard time starting her assignment to draw the jungle. She keeps making mistakes and getting teased until she decides to fix her picture by making it a night scene. (themes: self-esteem, uniqueness, problem-solving) Show #202

The Relatives Came
by Cynthia Rylant
Illustrated by Stephen Gammell
It is summer and time for a visit with the relatives, who come up from Virginia and plant in the garden, fix things around the house, and generally get into everything until it is time to go home. (themes: family, sharing) Show #103

The Rooster Who Went to His Uncle's Wedding
by Alma Flor Ada
Illustrated by Kathleen Kuchera
The rooster is getting ready for his uncle's wedding when he stoops in the mud for a kernel of corn. This sets off a sequence of events involving the grass, a lamb, a dog, a stick, a campfire, a brook, and the sun. (themes: sequence of events, nature, animals, problem-solving) Show #125

Rose Meets Mr. Wintergarten
by Bob Graham
Rose Summer befriends her scary neighbor, Mr. Wintergarten, when her ball is accidentally tossed into his yard and she goes to get it back. (themes: friendship, feelings [fear]) Show #101

Rosie's Baby Tooth
by Maryann MacDonald
Illustrated by Melissa Sweet
Rosie's baby tooth has fallen out, but she doesn't want to give it up. She writes to the tooth fairy, who leaves a new gold chain under her pillow so Rosie can keep the tooth forever. (themes: family, identity [growing up]) Show #129

The Rough-Face Girl
by Rafe Martin
Illustrated by David Shannon
In this Native American version of the Cinderella story, the Rough-Face Girl wins the hand of the Invisible Being because she is the only one able to recognize him in the beautiful nature around them. (themes: fairy tale, identity) Show #114

Ruby, the Copy Cat
by Peggy Rathmann
Ruby is the new girl at school who wants so badly to fit in that she copies everything that Angela says and does. When Angela gets angry, their teacher encourages Ruby to show everyone that she is special too by sharing her talent for hopping. (themes: friendship, uniqueness) Show #122

Rumpelstiltskin retold and illustrated by Paul O. Zelinsky
In this classic fairy tale, a miller's daughter is forced to spin straw into gold and agrees to the help of a strange little man in exchange for her firstborn child. When the girl succeeds, marries the prince, and bears a son, the man threatens to collect on his deal unless she can guess his name. When her servant overhears the little man's name in the woods, the deal is off and the baby is saved. (themes: fairy tale, resourcefulness) Show #109

The Seven Chinese Brothers
by Margaret Mahy
Illustrated by Jean and Mou-Sien Tseng
Seven brothers in China have special supernatural powers that allow them to help each other in times of danger and need. One by one they help defend each other from the evil Emperor until they are all reunited at the Great Wall. (themes: family [siblings], resourcefulness, cooperation) Show #128

Sheila Rae, the Brave
by Kevin Henkes
Sheila Rae is not afraid of anything, but one day, she decides to walk home a new way and gets lost. She is overcome by fear until her little sister Louise, who has followed her, comes to the rescue and leads them both home. (themes: family [siblings], feelings [fear, courage]) Show #210

alphabetical booklist

The Shepherd Boy
by Kristine L. Franklin
Illustrated by Jill Kastner
A young shepherd boy in the Southwest leads his herd of fifty sheep through the canyon to drink at a secret spring. When he finds one day that one of them is missing, he goes back through the canyon, where he finds a little lamb lost in the ancient cave village. (themes: responsibility, animals) Show #219

Slither McCreep and His Brother Joe by Tony Johnston
Illustrated by Victoria Chess
When Joe the snake refuses to share his toys one day, his brother Slither retaliates by squeezing each one of them until they break. His mother sends him to his room, where, after some time to reflect, he breaks his piggy bank in order to replace the broken toys. (themes: family [siblings], sharing, responsibility) Show #135

Socrates
by Rascal and Gert Bogaerts
Socrates is a lonely dog who lives alone on the streets and dreams of having a friend until the day he finds a pair of glasses and puts them on. Now people are friendlier, and when he meets the original owner of the glasses, a street musician, Socrates finds a new home with him. (themes: friendship, sharing) Show #125

A Special Trade by Sally Wittman
Pictures by Karen Gundersheimer
Bartholomew is Nellie's older neighbor, who has helped to care for her since she was a baby, taking her for walks in her carriage and picking her up as she learned to skate. When Bartholomew falls down the stairs and returns from the hospital in a wheelchair, it is time for Nellie to take care of him, helping him get up and taking him for walks. (themes: friendship, caring/concern for others) Show #140

"Stand Back," Said the Elephant, "I'm Going to Sneeze!"
by Patricia Thomas
Pictures by Wallace Tripp
A little mouse saves the day by scaring the elephant who was about to sneeze and cause a disastrous windstorm. But when the big elephant starts to laugh, the earth begins to shake. (themes: rhyme, animals, cause and effect) Show #140

Stina by Lena Anderson
While staying with her grandfather at the ocean on her annual summer trip, Stina learns the right way to experience a storm, properly dressed and with someone else. Together, they explore the aftermath of the storm on the beach, and Stina finds a special box to hold her summer treasures. (themes: family [grandfather], feelings [fear, curiosity], nature) Show #113

Stop That Pickle! by Peter Armour
Illustrated by Andrew Shachat
When the last pickle jumps from the jar at Mr. Adolf's deli, a growing number of different foods join along in the race to catch him until he collides with a very young boy. When the pickle cries, the boy decides to eat all the other foods, finishing up with the ice cream, which just doesn't go with a sour pickle, so the pickle is spared. (themes: adventure, sequence of events) Show #208

Stories to Tell from **Meet Danitra Brown** by Nikki Grimes
Illustrated by Floyd Cooper
In a poem, a little girl admires her friend, Danitra, who wants to win the Nobel Prize. (themes: friendship, self-esteem) Show #214

Storm Boy written and illustrated by Paul Owen Lewis
A Native American chief's son is lost in a storm and finds himself in a new village where he learns about some new traditions. When the host chief helps him with a magic trip home, he finds that he has been gone for one year. (themes: fantasy, differences, feelings [homesickness]) Show #302

The Story of a Boy Named Will, Who Went Sledding Down the Hill
by Daniil Kharms, translated by Jamey Gambrell
Illustrated by Vladimir Radunsky
A boy named Will starts down the hill on his sled, bumping into a hunter and a series of animals who come along for the ride. (themes: adventure, sequence of events) Show #206

The Story of Ferdinand
by Munro Leaf
Illustrated by Robert Lawson
When Ferdinand, the unusually gentle bull, is stung by a bee one day and jumps and snorts in pain, he is selected for the bullfights in Madrid. But on the day of the big fight, he only sits in the center of the ring and is returned to his favorite spot under the cork tree. (themes: uniqueness, animals) Show #107

Subway Sparrow by Leyla Torres
When a sparrow flies into a subway car, three riders manage to help her escape, though none of them speak the same language. (themes: cooperation, problem-solving) Show #205

Suddenly! written and illustrated by Colin McNaughton
Preston walks along, oblivious to the fact that he is being followed by a hungry wolf, and manages to escape only by a series of sudden changes in plans. (themes: cause and effect, interactive) Show #304

Super Dooper Jezebel
by Tony Ross
Super Dooper Jezebel is so perfect in every way that she gets a medal from the President, a statue is erected in her honor, and she goes on television to talk about herself. But one day, while telling the other children to walk, not run, she is snapped up by the crocodile they are fleeing, who has escaped from the zoo. (theme: uniqueness) Show #138

Swamp Angel by Anne Isaacs
Illustrated by Paul O. Zelinsky
Swamp Angel wrestles Thundering Tarnation, a huge bear, to save the winter supplies of Tennessee settlers in an original tall tale. (themes: fairy tale, problem-solving, sharing) Show #208

That's Good! That's Bad!
by Margery Cuyler
Illustrated by David Catrow
While on a visit to the zoo with his parents, a little boy is carried up into the sky by his balloon, which carries him through a series of accidents and near misses where things that seem bad are actually good and things that seem good only lead to more bad. Finally, he is snatched up by a stork who carries him back to his parents at the zoo. (themes: fantasy, adventure, sequence of events, interactive) Show #111

This and That by Jules Sykes
Illustrated by Tanya Linch
Curious about why Cat has asked to borrow something from each of them, her animal friends follow her to the stable, where they find two new kittens in a nest made from the things that she borrowed. (themes: friendship, sharing, feelings [generosity], animals, resourcefulness, interactive)** Show #305

alphabetical booklist

The Three Little Wolves and the Big Bad Pig by Eugene Trivizas Illustrated by Helen Oxenbury
In this variation on *The Three Little Pigs*, three cuddly wolves build a series of houses that are each destroyed by the big bad pig. Finally, when they build a fragile house of flowers, the pig is overcome by its beauty, comes in for tea, and moves in to stay. (themes: fairy tale, friendship, feelings [surprise]) Show #201

Three Wishes by Lucille Clifton Illustrated by Michael Hays
While playing with her friend Victorius on New Year's Day, Zenobia finds a penny with her birth year on it, which entitles her to three wishes. After wasting the first two wishes, she learns an important lesson about friendship and uses the third wish more wisely. (themes: feelings [anger], friendship, fantasy) Show #105

The Tickleoctopus by Audrey Wood Illustrated by Don Wood
Millions of years ago, Bup the prehistoric boy lived with his ill-tempered parents and was forced to do all the chores by himself, because his other siblings are missing. Then one day, out of their cave pond emerges the Tickleoctopus, who teaches the unhappy people to laugh and smile and helps them to find the lost children. (themes: family, feelings [happiness], fairy tale) Show #204

Time Train by Paul Fleischman Illustrated by Claire Ewart
On a class trip to study dinosaurs out west, a group of schoolchildren and their teacher find themselves on an express train going back in time, where they have the opportunity to meet and play with real dinosaurs. (themes: imagination, nature, adventure) Show #207

Timothy Goes to School by Rosemary Wells
When Timothy starts a new school, he always seems to be wearing the wrong thing, and Claude, who is always dressed just right, always teases him. Timothy doesn't want to go back to school until the day he meets Violet, who is jealous of another little girl who seems to do everything right. (themes: friendship, feelings [jealousy, teasing]) Show #109

Too Many Tamales by Gary Soto Illustrated by Ed Martinez
Maria and her mother are making tamales for their big Christmas celebration with the relatives when she secretly tries on Mama's beautiful ring. Then, thinking she has lost it in the batter, she and her cousins eat all 24 tamales to try to get it back. When she finds it back on her mother's finger, all the relatives pitch in to make a new batch of tamales. (themes: family, holidays [Christmas], problem-solving) Show #211

Tops & Bottoms adapted and illustrated by Janet Stevens
A poor but clever rabbit outsmarts a lazy and rich bear by making a deal to work his land in exchange for part of the crop. When the hardworking rabbit comes out with the best of the crop after three harvests, he is able to start his own vegetable stand, and the bear finally realizes it is time to get to work. (themes: sharing, resourcefulness, nature) Show #220

The Treasure by Uri Shulevitz
After dreaming three times about a treasure under a bridge near the royal palace in the capital city, a poor man named Isaac sets out to find it. When he arrives at the bridge, one of the guards there laughingly tells him of his dream to look in a pot under the stove of a poor old man. When Isaac returns home to discover the treasure under the stove, he uses the money to build a house of prayer. (themes: determination, feelings [hope], sharing) Show #124

The Trouble with Mom by Babette Cole
The other parents decide that their children should no longer play at Mom's house because she is too different — she wears funny hats, rides on a broomstick, and doesn't get along with the other parents at school, whom she turns into frogs. They change their minds when Mom uses her magic powers to put out a fire at the school, saving all their children. (themes: family [mother], differences) Show #117

The True Story of the Three Little Pigs by A. Wolf as told to Jon Scieszka Illustrated by Lane Smith
In the wolf's version of the classic tale, the wolf tells a wild tale about how a big sneeze and an innocent request started all his troubles with the three little pigs. (themes: fairy tale, differences [perspective]) Show #201

'Twas the Night Before Thanksgiving written and illustrated by Dav Pilkey
Schoolchildren on a field trip to Mack Nugget's farm save the lives of eight turkeys in this Thanksgiving version of the classic Christmas poem. (themes: holidays [Thanksgiving], friendship, sharing, caring/concern for others) Show #310

Twist with a Burger, Jitter with a Bug by Linda Lowery Illustrated by Pat Dypold
This colorful book celebrates dance as images and animals dance across the pages in a variety of exuberant ways. (themes: nature, music, fantasy, rhyme) Show #303

Two Badd Babies by Jeffie R. Gordon Illustrated by Chris L. Demarest
Two babies are put down for their nap, but they're not tired. They rock and bounce their crib so much it rolls them all over town, taking them to the bakery for pastry, to the movies, out for a hamburger, on a visit to their father's bookstore, and then finally back home for their nap. (themes: fantasy, adventure) Show #115

Two of Everything by Lily Toy Hong
When an old and poor couple discover a magic pot that creates an identical double of anything that is dropped in, they multiply their meager wealth and become rich. Then the wife is accidentally knocked inside, and her double comes out. She is furious until the husband is knocked in, and the two couples are able to live together side by side. (themes: fairy tale, problem-solving) Show #108

Uncle Jed's Barbershop by Margaree King Mitchell Illustrated by James Ransome
A little girl tells the story of her Uncle Jed, the only black barber in the county, who travels from town to town giving haircuts, and his determination to open his own barbershop, which he finally does at the end of his life. (themes: determination, family, self-esteem, feelings [disappointment, love]) Show #214

The Very Quiet Cricket by Eric Carle
A new cricket tries desperately to make a noise in response to the greetings of the other insects, but no matter how much he rubs his wings together, he cannot make a sound — until he meets another cricket and responds with a chirp. (themes: determination, sounds, nature, identity)** Show #106

We Could Be Friends from *I Like You, If You Like Me* by Myra Cohn Livingston
This short poem is about the things that friends do together. (theme: friendship) Show #221

alphabetical booklist

The Whales' Song by Dyan Sheldon
Illustrated by Gary Blythe

Lily learns from her grandmother how to communicate with the whales in the ocean by leaving them special surprises in the water. (themes: family [grandmother], imagination, nature) Show #209

When the Fly Flew In . . .
by Lisa Westberg Peters
Pictures by Brad Sneed

A little boy can't clean his messy room because all the animals are asleep. Then a fly buzzes in and starts a sequence of events in which one by one each of the animals wakes up and does something to clean the room. (themes: imagination, animals, problem-solving, sequence of events)** Show #212

Whistle for Willie
by Ezra Jack Keats

Peter plays around his neighborhood and his house, trying hard to learn to whistle for his dog Willie. (themes: self-esteem, determination, sounds)** Show #106

Wilfrid Gordon McDonald Partridge by Mem Fox
Illustrated by Julie Vivas

When Wilfrid Gordon McDonald Partridge learns that his friend Miss Nancy from the rest home is losing her memory, he puts together some items that fit the descriptions of memory that the other adults give him. Each object brings back some part of the past for Miss Nancy, and in this way her memory is restored. (themes: friendship, caring/concern for others, feelings [generosity]) Show #107

Wilson Sat Alone by Debra Hess
Illustrated by Diane Greenseid

At school, Wilson sits, eats, reads, and plays alone until a new girl arrives at school and roars at Wilson, and to everyone's surprise, he roars back. From then on, Wilson is no longer alone. (theme: friendship) Show #221

Wind Says Goodnight
by Katy Rydell
Illustrated by David Jorgensen

One by one, the wind asks the different animals and things in the nighttime world to stop making noise so that the child can go to sleep. (themes: music, nature, sequence of events, problem-solving) Show #202

Winnie the Witch
by Valerie Thomas
Illustrated by Korky Paul

Winnie the Witch can never find her black cat inside her black house, so she tries turning him different colors. Nothing works until she solves her problem by turning him black again and putting colors all over her house. (themes: colors, problem-solving) Show #119

The Wolf's Chicken Stew
by Keiko Kasza

A wolf who loves to cook decides to fatten up a chicken for his stew by baking her delicious goodies, which he leaves on her stoop. But when it is time to cook the chicken, he is greeted by the grateful baby chicks, who thank him for his generosity and invite him to share their dinner. (themes: sharing, cause/effect) Show #123

The Woman Who Outshone the Sun based on a poem by Alejandro Cruz Martinez
Pictures by Fernando Olivera

A beautiful newcomer is driven from the village by suspicious townspeople because she is different. But when their fertile river follows her in her long flowing hair, they beg her to return and learn to accept her as one of them. (themes: fairy tale, differences) Show #132

Would You Rather . . .
by John Burningham

This picture book asks "would you rather," by presenting a variety of different choices, some good and some bad, about what the reader would rather do, or have, or be. (themes: rhyme, problem-solving [making choices]) Show #213

Thematic Booklist

Social/Emotional Themes

Caring/Concern for Others
Babushka Baba Yaga
Chicken Sunday
Courtney
Horton Hatches the Egg
The Hungry Thing
The Hunter
Maxi, the Hero
Mirette on the Highwire
Not So Fast, Songololo
The Perfect Orange: A Tale from Ethiopia
Prize in the Snow
A Special Trade
'Twas the Night Before Thanksgiving
Wilfrid Gordon McDonald Partridge

Cooperation
The Big Pumpkin
Contrary Mary
¿Donde Esta Mi Osito?
Farmer Duck
La Gallinita Roja
Greetings from Sandy Beach
How Many Days to America?
Hunting the White Cow
Listen, Buddy
The Little Red Hen
Mole's Hill
The Old Ladies Who Liked Cats
Playing Right Field
The Rat and the Tiger
The Seven Chinese Brothers
Subway Sparrow

Determination
Amber on the Mountain
The Art Lesson
Broderick
How Many Days to America?
Mirette on the Highwire
Pip's Magic
The Treasure
Uncle Jed's Barbershop
The Very Quiet Cricket
Whistle for Willie

Family
Baby Rattlesnake
A Big Fat Enormous Lie
The Boy and the Ghost
The Cat Who Lost His Purr
Chicken Sunday
Cuddly Dudley
The Dragon of an Ordinary Family
Flower Garden
Greetings from Sandy Beach
The Hunter
Jessica
More, More, More, Said the Baby
Morris's Disappearing Bag
Night Tree
Noisy Nora
Over the River and Through the Woods
Possum Come A-Knockin'
The Relatives Came
Rosie's Baby Tooth
The Tickleoctopus
Too Many Tamales
Uncle Jed's Barbershop

Mother
The Baby Blue Cat Who Said No
The Big Big Sea
Contrary Mary
Froggy Gets Dressed
Honey Paw and Lightfoot
I Hear a Noise
Is Your Mama a Llama?
Jonathan and His Mommy
Mama, Do You Love Me?
Monster Mama
A Mother for Choco
My Mama Had a Dancing Heart
My Mom Is Excellent
Owl Babies
The Trouble with Mom

Father
First Pink Light
Gorilla
The Painter

Grandmother
Abuela
Babushka Baba Yaga
Nathaniel Willy, Scared Silly
Not So Fast, Songololo
The Paper Princess

Grandfather
Grandpa's Face
The Gullywasher
Stina

Siblings
Cabbage Rose
The Ghost-Eye Tree
Julius, the Baby of the World
The Magic House
My Little Brother
Ollie Knows Everything
One of Three
The Seven Chinese Brothers
Sheila Rae, the Brave
Slither McCreep and His Brother Joe

Feelings
Aunt Isabel Tells a Good One
Maggie and the Pirate

Anger
Five Bad Boys, Billy Que and the Dustdobbin
Three Wishes

Being Left Out
Noisy Nora
One of Three

Comfort
Baby Rattlesnake
A Mother for Choco
Owl Babies
Courage
The Banza
The Boy and the Ghost
Do Not Open
The Ghost-Eye Tree
Ghost's Hour, Spook's Hour
The Little Old Lady Who Was Not Afraid of Anything
Pip's Magic
Sheila Rae, the Brave

thematic booklist

Curiosity
Do Not Open
Stina

Disappointment
Uncle Jed's Barbershop

Embarrassment
Chrysanthemum
A Porcupine Named Fluffy

Excitement
First Pink Light

Fear
The Amazing Bone
¿Donde Esta Mi Osito?
Franklin in the Dark
The Ghost-Eye Tree
Ghost's Hour, Spook's Hour
Go Away, Big Green Monster!
Grandpa's Face
The House That Drac Built
I Hear a Noise
I'm Coming to Get You!
Ira Sleeps Over
It's the Bear!
Little Lumpty
The Little Mouse, the Red Ripe Strawberry and the Big Hungry Bear
The Little Old Lady Who Was Not Afraid of Anything
Nathaniel Willy Scared Silly
Ollie Knows Everything
Owl Babies
Pip's Magic
Rose Meets Mr. Wintergarten
Sheila Rae, the Brave
Stina

Generosity
Fairy Went A-Marketing
The Perfect Orange: A Tale from Ethiopia
This and That
Wilfred Gordon McDonald Partridge

Greed
Magic Spring
The Monkey and the Crocodile
The Perfect Orange: A Tale from Ethiopia

Happiness
Dogteam
Life Is Fun
My Mama Had a Dancing Heart
The Tickleoctopus

Homesickness
Going Home
Storm Boy

Hope
How Many Days to America?
The Treasure

Jealousy
Julius, the Baby of the World
Timothy Goes to School

Loneliness
Babushka Baba Yaga
Gorilla
Miss Spider's Tea Party

Love
Contrary Mary
Grandpa's Face
Julius, the Baby of the World
Mama, Do You Love Me?
The Man Who Kept His Heart in a Bucket
Monster Mama
My Little Brother
Uncle Jed's Barbershop

Relief
I'm Coming to Get You!
My Little Brother
Ollie Knows Everything

Sadness
Eddie and Teddy
The Old Dog
Owl Babies

Surprise
The Three Little Wolves and the Big Bad Pig

Teasing
Chrysanthemum
Monster Mama
Timothy Goes to School

Vanity
The Emperor's New Clothes

Friendship

The Adventures of Taxi Dog
Amber on the Mountain
Annie Bananie
Babushka Baba Yaga
The Banza
The Big Pumpkin
Boodil, My Dog
Chicken Sunday
Courtney
Don't Fidget a Feather
The Doorbell Rang
Earl's Too Cool for Me
Eddie and Teddy
Elmer
Going Home
The Happy Hedgehog Band
Hi!
Ira Sleeps Over
Jessica
Lady Bugatti
The Last Time I Saw Harris
Maebelle's Suitcase
Maggie and the Pirate
The Man Who Kept His Heart in a Bucket
Mirette on the Highwire
Miss Spider's Tea Party
Mouse's Birthday
The Old Dog
The Paper Princess
A Porcupine Named Fluffy
The Rat and the Tiger
Rose Meets Mr. Wintergarten
Ruby, the Copy Cat
Socrates
A Special Trade
Stories to Tell from Meet Danitra Brown
This and That
The Three Little Wolves and the Big Bad Pig
Three Wishes
Timothy Goes to School
'Twas the Night Before Thanksgiving
We Could Be Friends
Wilfrid Gordon McDonald Partridge
Wilson Sat Alone

Imagination

Abuela
A Big Fat Enormous Lie
Duckat
Going Home
The Gullywasher
If
Jessica
The Magic House
Time Train
The Whales' Song
When the Fly Flew In

Responsibility

Any Kind of Dog
Babushka's Doll
Baby Rattlesnake
A Big Fat Enormous Lie
The Boy and the Ghost
Clean Your Room Harvey Moon
The Empty Pot
A Flea in the Ear
Froggy Gets Dressed
La Gallinita Roja

thematic booklist

Goldilocks and the Three Bears
The Grasshopper and the Ants
Horton Hatches the Egg
Listen, Buddy
The Little Red Hen
The Mitten
The Shepherd Boy
Slither McCreep and His Brother Joe

Self-Esteem

Amazing Grace
Bear
Chrysanthemum
The Fish Who Could Wish
Little Peep
Playing Right Field
A Porcupine Named Fluffy
Regina's Big Mistake
Stories to Tell from Meet Danitra Brown
Uncle Jed's Barbershop
Whistle for Willie

Sharing

The Big Pumpkin
Company's Coming
The Doorbell Rang
Flower Garden
The Grasshopper and the Ants
Knock, Knock, Teremok!
The Leopard's Drum
The Little Mouse, the Red Ripe Strawberry and the Big
    Hungry Bear
Mole's Hill
Monster Mama
Morris's Disappearing Bag
Night Tree
Over the River and Through the Woods
The Painter
The Perfect Orange: A Tale from Ethiopia
The Relatives Came
Slither McCreep and His Brother Joe
Socrates
Swamp Angel
This and That
The Treasure
'Twas the Night Before Thanksgiving
The Wolf's Chicken Stew

Cognitive Themes

Alphabet

Chicka Chicka Boom Boom
The Folks in the Valley

Animals

All Pigs Are Beautiful
Any Kind of Dog
Bear
Boodil, My Dog
The Cat Who Lost His Purr
Courtney
Dinner at the Panda Palace
Dogteam
Duckat
A Flea in the Ear
The Happy Day
Honey Paw and Lightfoot
Horton Hatches the Egg
Is Your Mama a Llama?
Lady Bugatti
The Leopard's Drum
Little Peep
Little Polar Bear
The Mitten
Mole's Hill
The Monkey and the Crocodile
A Mother for Choco
Nathaniel Willy, Scared Silly
Nothing at All
The Old Dog
Owl Eyes
The Rooster Who Went to His Uncle's Wedding
The Shepherd Boy
"Stand Back," Said the Elephant, "I'm Going to Sneeze!"
The Story of Ferdinand
This and That
When the Fly Flew In

Cause and Effect

Little Peep
"Stand Back," Said the Elephant, "I'm Going to Sneeze!"
Suddenly!
The Wolf's Chicken Stew

Colors

Elmer
Go Away, Big Green Monster!
The Happy Day
The Last Time I Saw Harris
Winnie the Witch

Counting

Dinner at the Panda Palace
The Doorbell Rang
Miss Spider's Tea Party

Music

Frog Went A-Courtin'
The Grasshopper and the Ants
The Happy Hedgehog Band
The Itsy Bitsy Spider
Night Tree
Twist with a Burger, Jitter with a Bug
Wind Says Goodnight

Nature

All Pigs Are Beautiful
Bear
The Big Big Sea
Dear Mr. Blueberry
Dogteam
Effie
The Empty Pot
Flower Garden
The Gullywasher
The Happy Day
Honey Paw and Lightfoot
A House is a House for Me
The Hunter
The Itsy Bitsy Spider
My Little Red Car
My Mama Had a Dancing Heart
Night Tree
The Old Ladies Who Liked Cats
Prize in the Snow
The Rooster Who Went to His Uncle's Wedding
Stina
Time Train
Tops & Bottoms
Twist with a Burger, Jitter with a Bug
The Very Quiet Cricket
The Whales' Song
Wind Says Goodnight

Opposites

Contrary Mary

Sequence of Events

Donna O'Neeshuck Was Chased by Some Cows
The House That Drac Built
If You Give a Mouse a Cookie
King Bidgood's in the Bathtub
Knock, Knock, Teremok!
The Mitten
The Old Ladies Who Liked Cats
Possum Come A-Knockin'

thematic booklist

Pug, Slug and Doug the Thug
The Rooster Who Went to His Uncle's Wedding
Stop That Pickle!
The Story of a Boy Named Will, Who Went Sledding Down the Hill
That's Good! That's Bad!
When the Fly Flew In
Wind Says Goodnight

Shapes
Go Away, Big Green Monster!

Size
Five Bad Boys, Billy Que and the Dustdobbin
Goldilocks and the Three Bears
I'm Coming to Get You!
Mouse's Birthday
The Rat and the Tiger

Sounds
The Cat Who Lost His Purr
Chicka Chicka Boom Boom
Ghost's Hour, Spook's Hour
Nothing at All
The Very Quiet Cricket
Whistle for Willie

Vocabulary
A House is a House for Me
Lady Bugatti

Cultural/Social Diversity Themes

Differences
Amazing Grace
Babushka Baba Yaga
Chicken Sunday
Company's Coming
Courtney
Duckat
Effie
Elmer
Elvira
Englebert the Elephant
The Folks in the Valley
Franklin in the Dark
More, More, More, Said the Baby
A Mother for Choco
The Paper Princess
Storm Boy
The Trouble with Mom
The True Story of the Three Little Pigs
The Woman Who Outshone the Sun

Holidays

Christmas
Night Tree
Too Many Tamales

Halloween
The Big Pumpkin
The House That Drac Built
The Little Old Lady Who Was Not Afraid of Anything
Halloween Howls: Riddles That Are a Scream

Thanksgiving
How Many Days to America?
Over the River and Through the Woods
'Twas the Night Before Thanksgiving

Identity
Broderick
Daley B
Duckat
Elvira
The Emperor's New Clothes
Green Wilma
Is Your Mama a Llama?
Jonathan and His Mommy
A Porcupine Named Fluffy
Rosie's Baby Tooth
The Rough-Face Girl
The Very Quiet Cricket

Uniqueness
Amazing Grace
The Art Lesson
The Baby Blue Cat Who Said No
Boodil, My Dog
The Boy with Square Eyes
Cabbage Rose
Elmer
Elvira
The Fish Who Could Wish
Princess Smartypants
Regina's Big Mistake
Ruby, the Copy Cat
The Story of Ferdinand
Super Dooper Jezebel

Critical Thinking/Problem-Solving Themes

Problem-Solving
Alistair's Elephant
The Big Pumpkin
The Boy with Square Eyes
Daley B
¿Donde Esta Mi Osito?

Effie
A Flea in the Ear
Franklin in the Dark
The Grumpalump
A Hat for Minerva Louise
The Hungry Thing
Hunting the White Cow
King Bidgood's in the Bathtub
Knock, Knock, Teremok!
The Leopard's Drum
The Little Old Lady Who Was Not Afraid of Anything
Maebelle's Suitcase
Ming Lo Moves the Mountain
Mole's Hill
Nathaniel Willy, Scared Silly
Ollie Knows Everything
Regina's Big Mistake
The Rooster Who Went to His Uncle's Wedding
Subway Sparrow
Swamp Angel
Too Many Tamales
Two of Everything
When the Fly Flew In
Wind Says Goodnight
Winnie the Witch
Would You Rather . . .

Resourcefulness
Amber on the Mountain
Bear
Borreguita and the Coyote
Chicken Sunday
Franklin in the Dark
The Gingerbread Man
The Happy Hedgehog Band
A Hat for Minerva Louise
Honey Paw and Lightfoot
How Many Days to America?
The Leopard's Drum
The Little Old Lady Who Was Not Afraid of Anything
The Monkey and the Crocodile
The Old Ladies Who Liked Cats
Pug, Slug and Doug the Thug
Rumpelstiltskin
The Seven Chinese Brothers
This and That
Tops & Bottoms

thematic booklist

Types of Stories

Adventure

Abuela
The Adventures of Taxi Dog
Aunt Isabel Tells a Good One
Buz
Cuddly Dudley
Donna O'Neeshuck Was Chased by Some Cows
Englebert the Elephant
The Ghost-Eye Tree
Going Home
Greetings from Sandy Beach
A Hat for Minerva Louise
How Many Days to America?
The Hunter
The Last Time I Saw Harris
Little Lumpty
Little Polar Bear
My Little Red Car
The Paper Princess
Stop That Pickle!
The Story of a Boy Named Will, Who Went Sledding Down the Hill
That's Good! That's Bad!
Time Train
Two Badd Babies

Fairy Tales

Babushka Baba Yaga
The Banza
Borreguita and the Coyote
Cabbage Rose
The Emperor's New Clothes
The Fortune-Tellers
The Gingerbread Man
Goldilocks and the Three Bears
The Leopard's Drum
Little Lumpty
Magic Spring
The Man Who Kept His Heart in a Bucket
Ming Lo Moves the Mountain
Owl Eyes
The Perfect Orange: A Tale from Ethiopia
Princess Smartypants
The Rough-Face Girl
Rumpelstiltskin
Swamp Angel
The Three Little Wolves and the Big Bad Pig
The Tickleoctopus
The True Story of the Three Little Pigs
Two of Everything
The Woman Who Outshone the Sun

Fantasy

Alistair's Elephant
The Amazing Bone
Anna and the Little Green Dragon
Babushka's Doll
The Big Pumpkin
The Boy and the Ghost
Buz
Dear Mr. Blueberry
Do Not Open
The Dragon of an Ordinary Family
Five Bad Boys, Billy Que and the Dustdobbin
Gorilla
Green Wilma
The Gullywasher
The House That Drac Built
I Hear a Noise
If
I'm Coming to Get You!
The Little Old Lady Who Was Not Afraid of Anything
Pigs Aplenty, Pigs Galore!
Storm Boy
That's Good! That's Bad!
Three Wishes
Twist with a Burger, Jitter with a Bug
Two Badd Babies

Interactive

The Baby Blue Cat Who Said No
The Doorbell Rang
Earl's Too Cool for Me
Hi!
Is Your Mama a Llama?
King Bidgood's in the Bathtub
Nothing at All
Suddenly!
That's Good! That's Bad!
This and That

Rhyme

The Adventures of Taxi Dog
Annie Bananie
Clean Your Room, Harvey Moon
Dinner at the Panda Palace
Donna O'Neeshuck Was Chased by Some Cows
Earl's Too Cool for Me
Englebert the Elephant
Frog Went A-Courtin'
The Grumpalump
Halloween Howls: Riddles That Are a Scream
A House is a House for Me
The Hungry Thing
Is Your Mama a Llama?
It's the Bear!
Jamberry
Maxi, the Hero
Miss Spider's Tea Party
Mouse's Birthday
Noisy Nora
Over the River and Through the Woods
Pigs Aplenty, Pigs Galore!
Playing Right Field
"Stand Back," Said the Elephant, "I'm Going to Sneeze!"
Twist with a Burger, Jitter with a Bug
Would You Rather . . .

Appropriate Books for 2- and 3-Year-Olds

This is a list of books featured on *Storytime* that are particularly appropriate to read to younger children. The list includes stories that repeat catchy phrases, concept books including counting, color and shape books, and some rhyming and/or interactive books.

The Big Big Sea
Chicka Chicka Boom Boom
Contrary Mary
Dinner at the Panda Palace
The Doorbell Rang
Go Away, Big Green Monster!
The Happy Day
A Hat for Minerva Louise
Hi!
Is Your Mama a Llama?
It's the Bear
The Itsy Bitsy Spider
Jamberry
Jonathan and His Mommy
Mama, Do You Love Me?
More, More, More, Said the Baby
Mouse's Birthday
My Mom Is Excellent
Nothing at All
This and That
The Very Quiet Cricket
When the Fly Flew In
Whistle for Willie

Research Findings About Literacy

Overview

There are many strategies, philosophies, and disagreements about the best way to teach children to become competent readers. Whatever approach is followed, all educators agree that literacy is one of the keys to a successful life. What follows is a brief and simplified summary of findings from the most current research.

WHAT IS THE LINK BETWEEN THE HOME ENVIRONMENT AND LITERACY?

Every child comes to school with different abilities and knowledge about literacy and reading. Some of this is developmental, and some of this may have to do with the way parents or primary caregivers interact with children when they talk and when they read stories together. The following are ways in which you can help create a lifetime bond with reading for the children in your care:

Actively Reading
Actively involve children in the stories you read to them. Ask questions; ask them to predict what will happen next or to point to long or difficult words.

Using Language
Be responsive when children speak. Clarify or restate what a child says, and expand on it. Children who become early readers have a common link of parents and caregivers who speak with them in interactive ways during mealtime and during story reading time.

Sharing Reading Time
Literacy has less to do with how "print rich" the child's environment is and more to do with a parent's or caregiver's ability to involve children in the literacy experiences provided. Create a time when adults and children read separately but in the same room. Read and explore books as often as possible.

WHAT MOTIVATES CHILDREN TO READ?

Early Exposure
It is never too early to start sharing language and books with children. At least twelve different studies in the last two decades have shown that early experiences with literature can have a positive effect on children's attitudes toward reading and learning to read.

Appropriate Literature
Numerous studies have proven that exposure to literature will encourage children to read and write and strive to be as creative as the various authors they are exposed to. In addition, as children come to understand that there is meaning within the printed word, they try to create that meaning for themselves. The reward of understanding (and enjoying) something serves as an important motivation for continued reading.

Related Activities
The best tasks are ones that provide a challenge to the learner, promote independence, encourage children to pursue their personal interests, and take place in a social context with appropriate guidance. For example, if you read a book in which cooking occurs, follow up with a cooking activity. If the story involves nature, take a walk in your neighborhood to see if you can spot things you read about. (Note: Each *Storytime* show has several suggested activities relating to the books that are read on the show.)

research findings about literacy

IS REREADING A STORY VALUABLE?

Yes! It increases children's enjoyment as well as their comprehension, vocabulary development, and thinking skills.

Increases Comprehension

Many studies conclude that reading the same story to children several times over a period of time can improve comprehension. Research even suggests that children have a better chance of success in later years if they are read to often in their preschool years.

Improves Vocabulary

In order to learn new vocabulary words, children must actively participate rather than passively listen during story reading. Encourage them to point to or label words and pictures that are being read. Show them new words and words that they may recognize from somewhere else. Even children with small vocabularies can increase their word knowledge after actively rereading stories.

Promotes Thinking Skills

Rereading books to children lets them become familiar with the language of an author so that they can compare different writing styles and books. Promote thinking skills by asking children questions when they have finished reading a book. What did they like or dislike? What happened in the beginning, middle, or end of a book? How else could the story have ended?

What Other Specific Strategies Have Researchers Identified to Aid Literacy Development?

- **Independence**
  Encourage children to take responsibility for their own learning.

- **Communication**
  Talk with other parents and caregivers to expand your understanding of which books are appropriate and which activities will be effective for children.

- **Responsiveness**
  Answer questions, talk with children, and engage in non-verbal interchanges to help children develop better literacy and cognitive skills.

- **Involving Children**
  to make reading more enjoyable and to help improve their thinking and verbal skills.

- **Questions**
  Ask children to evaluate the cause and effect, look for similarities and differences, or identify a sequence of events and think of logical alternatives to a scenario, to help them develop thinking skills.

Glossary of Literacy Terms

Many words are used to describe the process of literacy and the tools used to promote it. Here are just a few to help you in your work.

ADVENTURE STORY
A story in which characters participate in a wonderful adventure. An adventure story can be fantasy, fiction, or science fiction.

CONCEPT BOOK
A book, in picture format, that is all about one concept, such as shapes, numbers, or colors.

CONNECTIONIST THEORY
A philosophy that promotes the belief that learning to read is a specific, teachable skill with an emphasis on learning the letters of the alphabet and how to recognize words through direct, teacher-led instruction. Once decoding of letters and words becomes automatic, connectionists think that students will be able to understand what they are reading. Advocates of this approach do not believe that it is enough for children to be in a print-rich environment.

CRITICAL THEORY
Similar to Social Constructivist theory. An approach that proposes that children can acquire literacy easier when the home and school cultures are similar. Advocates of this approach say that literacy learning is closely related to identity formation and that children have trouble with literacy when their home and school environments are too different.

EMERGENT LITERACY
Assumes that children try to create meaning from infancy. Therefore, early interactions with books and print and beginning attempts at making marks constitute steps in literacy development — attempts to read and write. The sum of these experiences is identified as emergent literacy — children's knowledge about reading and writing before they actually have the skills. Children have the potential to know that print means something, and their knowledge of reading is considered to include such things as knowing how to hold a book and understanding that letters separated by spaces are words and that stories have their own language and structure. A child who is exposed to a print-rich environment in which he or she sees signs, labels, letters, and, of course, books, is better positioned to acquire literacy.

ENVIRONMENTAL PRINT
The print that surrounds each of us daily. It includes posters on walls, magazines on coffee tables, notes and pictures on the refrigerator, labels and signs, logos and symbols.

FAIRY TALE
A classic, age-old story that has passed from generation to generation, often with adaptations made over time.

FAMILY LITERACY
Involves the transfer of information and attitudes from generation to generation. Since literacy development is a social process, it necessarily requires family involvement and support. Activities such as reading to a child; having books, magazines, and catalogues in the home; and seeing adults using print contribute to the child's interest and motivation. Parents and teachers can promote family literacy activities by sending books home with children, creating literacy projects that involve the family, and sharing information with families.

FANTASY
Imaginative stories in which the action takes place in nonexistent, unreal worlds with incredible characters. Its primary purpose is to entertain.

FICTION
Invented stories that are created with the primary goal of entertainment and the secondary goal of instruction to the audience. The key to fiction is that it makes readers think and, more importantly, feel. Such stories are great for children to begin to develop emotional bonds with books. (Examples: fables, novels, fairy tales, folklore.)

FUNCTIONAL ILLITERACY
People are considered functionally illiterate when they have severely limited reading and writing skills. Many times individuals with such limitations manage fairly well in society by using other strategies to compensate for their lack of skills.

ILLITERACY
Lack of reading and writing skills sufficient to successfully meet the needs and demands of adult life.

glossary of literacy terms

INTERACTIVE STORY
One in which the reader or listener is invited to participate by responding, touching, opening flaps, or otherwise physically or verbally interacting with the book. (You can make a story interactive by having children participate in the repetition of key phrases.)

INVENTED SPELLING
Comes before children learn conventional spelling. In their writing development, children spell words according to the sounds they hear. This allows children to feel empowered in being able to express themselves.

LITERACY
According to the National Literacy Act of 1991, an individual's ability to read, write, and speak in English and compute and solve problems at levels of proficiency necessary to function on the job and in society, to achieve one's goals, and to develop one's knowledge and potential.

MEDIA LITERACY
A field of education about the media (techniques, messages, tools of production, etc.) designed to empower viewers and consumers. It acknowledges that consumers must be active in decoding the media and aims to change how we respond and react to media. The goal is to demystify the media. A children's media literacy campaign might, for example, teach children how to look at ads on television—do the products do everything they say? Are the situations real? What are advertisers trying to do?

NONFICTION
Literature based on facts and reality. Nonfiction can contain fictional passages. (Examples: autobiographies, history chronicles.)

PHONICS
A traditional, bottom-up approach to learning to read that emphasizes that children have to understand and master the alphabetic principle. There is a code to be learned, and there is a series of sequential skills that need to be learned to become a reader. The phonics approach is best illustrated by the basal reader series. It should be noted that the majority of practitioners find the basic rules of phonics necessary to use in teaching reading.

REALISTIC FICTION
Stories in which everything in the story (characters, setting, plot) could happen to real people, but which don't have to be true stories. This type of fiction generally reflects current issues and cultural attitudes and can be controversial. Children identify with these stories through their own experiences and problems.

RHYME
A book in which the story is told in rhyme. The repetitive nature and predictability of rhymes is especially appealing to younger readers.

SCIENCE FICTION
Stories that draw imaginatively on science knowledge, theory, and speculation in plot, theme, setting, etc; a form of fantasy writing. Young children's science fiction often leads children on adventures to distant galaxies or parallel universes to meet aliens or other strange creatures.

SOCIAL CONSTRUCTIVISM
An area of research that states that language and literacy are acquired in a particular social and cultural context. Children learn about reading and how to read by interacting with each other and by absorbing the norms presented by the teacher. (For example: Stories are to be read in a comfortable setting; it is important to remember all the facts in a story.) Children will become more literate if they are taught texts that are meaningful to them. Children create meaning by responding to the text in a social setting with their words, their senses, and their emotions.

WHOLE LANGUAGE
A more recent approach to literacy. Literacy development begins with experiences and then moves into the individual pieces of those experiences. Reading and writing are seen as activities that occur throughout the day and feed each other's development. Whole language uses authentic books and involves writing experiences, such as letter writing, grocery lists, journals, etc.

WORDLESS BOOK
One in which there are pictures and no words, so that the readers can make up their own stories to accompany the pictures or simply identify what it is in the pictures.

Resources

Organizations

Laubach Literacy Action
U.S. Program of Laubach
Literacy International
Box 131
Syracuse, NY 13210
Telephone 315/422-9121

Provides volunteer tutors to and publications for adult new readers and limited English-speaking adults.

Literacy Volunteers of America Inc.
5795 Widewaters Parkway
Syracuse, NY 13214
Telephone 315/445-8000

Provides volunteer tutors to and publications for adult new readers and limited English-speaking adults.

National Center for Family Literacy
106 Promenade Court
Louisville, KY 40223
Telephone 502/327-7777

Sponsors family literacy programs offering basic education and literacy training for undereducated parents and preschool education for their young children, as well as parental support and intergenerational activities.

Reading Is Fundamental, Inc. (RIF)®
600 Maryland Ave. SW, Suite 600
Washington, DC 20024
Telephone 202/287-3220

Through a nationwide network of volunteer-run programs, RIF provides motivational reading activities and new books for children to choose and keep without cost to them or their families.

International Reading Association
800 Barksdale Road, PO Box 8139
Newark, DE 19714-8139
Telephone 302/731-1600

Through its publications provides information to parents and volunteer tutors about children's reading development.

Your School or Library

Librarians can recommend books, conduct story hours, and have a wealth of knowledge about children's literature.

Books and Videos

The Early Childhood Years: The 2- to 6-Year-Old, by Theresa and Frank Caplan, Bantam Books, 1983.

Excellent book about child development. Each phase includes information about language and literacy development, along with appropriate recommended books.

The Read-Aloud Handbook, by Jim Trelease, Penguin Books, 1995.

Good information about the benefits of reading aloud, including tips and recommended books.

For Reading Out Loud!: A Guide to Sharing Books With Children from Infancy to Teens, by Margaret Mary Kimmel and Elizabeth Segal, Dell, 1991.

Includes 400 book descriptions, an annotated bibliography, listening levels, and essays about reading.

Linking Literacy and Play, by Kathleen A. Roskos, Carol Vukelich, James F. Christie, Billie J. Enz, Susan B. Neuman, International Reading Association, 1995.

Provides ideas about how to use the natural environment of play to foster literacy development. Package includes one 12-minute video encased in a three-ring binder and one facilitator's guide within the binder.

Reading and Young Children: A Practical Guide for Child Care Providers, International Reading Association, 1992.

A ten-minute introductory training video for child care professionals and others who work with young children. Demonstrates techniques for reading aloud, choral reading, using Big Books, and storytelling, and suggests inexpensive resources to help child care facilities become "reader friendly."

Introducción a la Literatura Infantil y Juvenil, by Isabel Schon and Sarah Corona Berkin, International Reading Association, 1996.

Explores the many different types of Spanish language books available to young people. Chapters include comprehensive bibliographies of books listed at the appropriate reading level for beginning, intermediate, and young adult readers. Published in a Spanish language edition only.

resources

Book Talk and Beyond: Children and Teachers Respond to Literature, edited by Nancy L. Roser and Miriam G. Martinez, International Reading Association, 1995.

Demonstrates how to motivate and facilitate student literary discussions with book clubs, webbing and language charts, drama, and art.

Booklists: Children's Choices and Teachers' Choices, International Reading Association, 1996.

Listings of favorite books of school children and classroom teachers across the United States. Includes reading levels, annotations, and bibliographic data.

Teachers' Favorite Books for Kids: Teachers' Choices 1989-1993, International Reading Association, 1994.

A compilation of five years of Teachers' Choices lists. Books are grouped by reading levels. Annotations and bibliographic data are provided for each title, and indexes list books by title, author, and illustrator.

Magazines for Kids and Teens, revised edition, edited by Donald R. Stoll, International Reading Association and Educational Press Association of America, 1997.

Features descriptions of over 200 magazines and ordering information.

OUTREACH ADVISORY BOARD

Sharon Darling, President, National Center for Family Literacy

Patricia Edwards, Ph.D., Founder, Parents as Partners

Nancye Gaj, President, Motheread® Inc.

Ruth Graves, President, Reading Is Fundamental

Joan Irwin, Director of Publications, International Reading Association

Elizabeth Martinez, Executive Director, American Library Association

KCET COMMUNITY OUTREACH

Peter Rodriguez, Vice President, Community and Government Relations

Sharon Selico, Director, Community Relations and Outreach

Lynne Yancy Christian, Manager, Community Outreach

Patricia Smart, Outreach Coordinator

Sophia Woodard, Outreach Assistant

Bibliography

Anderson, R.C., Heibert, E.H., Scott, J.A., and Wilkinson, I.A.G. (1985). *Becoming a Nation of Readers: The Report of the Commision on Reading.* Washington, D.C.: National Academy of Education.

Bus, Adriana, and van Ijzendoorn, Marinus (1995). Research. The Netherlands.

Business Council for Effective Literacy Newsletter (April 1989). No. 19.

Calkins, L. (1986). *The Art of Teaching Writing.* Portsmouth, NH: Heinemann Educational Books.

Caplan, Theresa, and Caplan, Frank (1983). *The Early Childhood Years: The 2- to 6-Year-Old.* New York: Bantam Books.

Clay, M. (1979). Concepts about print tests, from *The Early Detection of Reading Difficulties.* New Zealand: Heinemann.

Crawford, Patricia A. (1995). "Early literacy: Emerging perspectives," *Journal of Research in Childhood Education,* 10 (1), 71-86.

Dickinson, D., Wolf, M., and Stotsky, S. (1993). "Words move: The interwoven development of oral and written language," in Gleason, J. B. (ed.), *The Development of Language.* New York: Macmillan Publishing Company.

Madura, Sandra (1995). "The line and texture of aesthetic response: Primary children study authors and illustrators." *The Reading Teacher,* 49 (2), 110-118.

Mason, J.M. (1992). *Reading Acquisition.*

National Reading Research Center (1994). *Study of Successful Strategies in Head Start Programs.*

Nespeca, S. (1996). "Literacy begins at home: Twenty-five ways to make sure reading runs in the family." *School Library Journal,* 42 (5), 25-29.

Norton, D. E. (1983). *Through the Eyes of a Child: Introduction to Children's Literature.* Toronto: Charles E. Merrill Publishing Company.

Senechal, Monique; Thomas, Eleanor; and Monker, Jo-Ann (1995). "Individual differences in 4-year-old children's acquisition of vocabulary during storybook reading," *Journal of Educational Psychology,* 87 (2), 218–229.

Shaw, H. (1972). *Dictionary of Literary Terms.* New York: McGraw-Hill Book Company.

Snow, Catherine, and Davidson, Rosalind (1995). Unpublished research study. Harvard Graduate School of Education.

Trelease, Jim (1995). *The Read-Aloud Handbook,* 4th ed. New York: Penguin Books.

Weaver, C. (1988/95). *Reading Process and Practice from Sociolinguistics to Whole Language.* Portsmouth, NH: Heinemann Educational Books.

Credits

This guide was developed by Media Education Consultants for KCET, Los Angeles, producers of *Storytime.*

Editors-In-Chief: Simone Bloom Nathan and Caren Keller Niss

Contributing Editors: Sharon Selico and Patricia Smart

Principal Writer: Anne F. Kaplan

Contributing Writers and Researchers: Cyrisse Jaffe, Pearl Mattenson, Kim Myers, Simone Bloom Nathan, Joshua Nathan, Caren Keller Niss, Faith Rogow

Copyeditors: GTS Graphics

Storytime is a production of KCET Los Angeles.

Storytime is made possible by a grant from Helen and Peter Bing. Additional funding for educational outreach in Southern California is provided by The Ahmanson Foundation.

Storytime is a children's television series broadcast on PBS.

© 1997 Community Television of Southern California. All Rights Reserved

Design: Greg Moraes Studio

Storytime Feedback Form

Storytime would like to hear from you. Your feedback about the television show and about this guide will help us better respond to your needs. Please complete and return this sheet to:

Storytime
KCET Community Outreach
4401 Sunset Boulevard
Los Angeles, CA 90027

THE TELEVISION SHOW

Watching *Storytime* exposes children to new books. ___ Agree ___ Disagree

I watch the television show. ___ Regularly ___ Occasionally ___ Never

The children enjoy the show. ___ Agree ___ Disagree

The children's favorite character is ___ Kino ___ Lucy ___ Mara ___ Celebrity guests

I have read *Storytime* books to children after seeing them on the show. ___ Agree ___ Disagree

Comments for the show's producers _____

_____

_____

_____

STORYTIME CONNECTIONS: A LITERACY RESOURCE GUIDE

I use the guide to give me ideas for books and activities. ___ Agree ___ Disagree

The guide has given me information I can use in my work. ___ Agree ___ Disagree

The most useful section of the guide is _____

The least useful section of the guide is _____

Additional comments and suggestions about the guide _____

_____

_____

_____

Call 800/336-READ (7323), extension 266 to order additional *Storytime* resource guides.